Sparking Change to Promote Equity

Sparking Change to Promote Equity illuminates the skills and practices that campus and district-level leaders of gifted and advanced programs need to encourage and support minoritized and marginalized student success in today's classrooms.

Designed to empower leaders and other educational stakeholders to build a more equitably represented student population within gifted and advanced programs, *Sparking Change* chapters offer a discourse on the benefit of incorporating culturally responsive gifted leadership practices to open the gateway toward recognizing, accepting and nurturing each gifted student according to their true needs, interests, challenges and abilities.By dismantling inequitable and oppressive systems that impede student potential, leaders can leverage CRGL behaviors to foster a more inclusive environment within advanced programs, allowing each student to flourish. In the context of the complexities of today's schools and advanced programs, this book provides recommendations and strategies towards developing an equitable leadership stance that is needing in gifted and advanced education.

Whether you're new to leadership, experienced, or an aspiring leader seeking to advance equity in gifted and advanced education, this book is a valuable resource for educational leaders to become more equitable in advanced level learning.

Dr. Javetta Jones Roberson serves as the District Coordinator of Secondary Advanced Academics & Gifted and Talented in McKinney ISD. She also serves as Lecturing Professor in the Teacher Education and Administration department at the University of North Texas. Her research interests include diverse gifted and Advanced Placement populations, equity in giftedness, culturally responsive pedagogy (teaching, leadership, and curriculum), and professional learning of teachers (special education and gifted).

T0383593

Dr. Kristina Henry Collins is the Executive Director for Robinson Center for Young Scholars at University of Washington (UW) in Seattle. At UW, she holds dual affiliate associate professor appointments in the College of Education at the Seattle and Tacoma campuses. Dr. Collins also continues to serve as a collaborating research fellow, mentor, and visiting professor for LBJ STEM Institute for STEM Education and Research at Texas State University.

Sparking Change to Promote Equity

Implementing Culturally Responsive Leadership Practices in Gifted and Advanced Programs

Javetta Jones Roberson and
Kristina Henry Collins

Routledge
Taylor & Francis Group

NEW YORK AND LONDON

Designed cover image: @getty

First published 2025

by Routledge
605 Third Avenue, New York, NY 10158

and by Routledge
4 Park Square, Milton Park, Abingdon, Oxon, OX14 4RN

Routledge is an imprint of the Taylor & Francis Group, an informa business

ISBN: 9781032449982 (hbk)
ISBN: 9781032448169 (pbk)
ISBN: 9781003374923 (ebk)

DOI: 10.4324/9781003374923

Typeset in Palatino
by Deanta Global Publishing Services, Chennai, India

Contents

Foreword

It is important to note that preparation and actions toward culturally responsive leadership in gifted and advanced programs is incredibly essential. Why? It is incredibly essential because it matters. It matters because historically in America, topics about cultural differences have too frequently been met with significant levels of challenge. It matters for the multiple reasons the authors clearly articulate in each chapter and topic in this book.

Roberson and Collins are to be commended by all who access *Sparking Change to Promote Equity: Implementing Culturally Responsive Leadership Practices in Gifted and Advanced Programs.* Their continuing quest to equip school-system leaders with appropriate skills to support racially, culturally, ethnically and linguistically different (RCELD) students is a success with this publication. The authors, through their very able and high levels of thought leadership knowledge, skills, abilities and experiences effectively demonstrate how this quest matters. This quest matters in its focus on culturally responsive leadership practice for general leadership in education, and particularly for leadership for gifted education and advanced academics.

I commend these fearless women for their passion to author such a publication. A publication on a topic such as culture, and more specifically on culturally responsive leadership within gifted learning, requires the highest levels of passion, or passionate behaviors, such as that which is possessed by these esteemed authors. Dr. Roberson and Dr. Collins, throughout their celebrated experiences, have met significant and several personal and professional tests of passion. In this context, their passionate behaviors are indeed required.

I am well aware and in awe of Dr. Roberson's and Dr. Collins' work. I have known and collaborated with them for many years. They demonstrate exemplary skills as true and genuine educational change agents across many contexts, particularly equity, diversity, inclusiveness and anti-racist contexts. A change agent regarding equity, diversity, inclusiveness and anti-racist contexts must possess passionate behaviors that are essential for transforming teaching and learning. They have exhibited these passionate behaviors through their boundless energy, boldness, courage, strength and deep feelings of enthusiasm toward cultivating the next generation of culturally responsive leaders. They are committed and excited about educational justice, righteousness and fairness with a quest to address our changing culturally diverse future. In that future, today's students will, as the authors posit, require certain tools. Students will require academic tools that accelerate learning, and that facilitate engagement, innovation and their sense of discovery. Students will also require *societal tools* that will positively maximize their respect and response to a culturally different world. It is critical therefore, that today's students have access to opportunities to allow them to actively participate in educational environments that are conceived and maintained by effective leaders, who passionately embrace and practice culturally responsive leadership.

Unfortunately, we are living in current times where some people in various segments of society are demonstrating racist-like attitudes that penalize diverse cultures. Rather than this segment of society choosing to focus on the more noble notion to dismantle racist attitudes, we see them orchestrating a disturbing flurry of attempts of cultural whitewashing. We see books being banned in schools' libraries, penalizing all students from each culture to learn about the ugly truths of America's past. This omittance is an outright contradiction in terms of what schools should promote and do. Schools are supposed to enlighten and enrich students. Schools exist to transform society and the world. This is one of the reasons this publication is extremely critical. *Sparking Change to Promote Equity* reveals the vision of these passionate authors who see the promises rather than penalties of a more diverse future and educational environment.

It focuses on students gaining access to and actively participating in appropriate learning environments. The learning environments will be realized only through effective, culturally responsive leadership with a focused intent of creating the best socially significant society and world that can be!

Furthermore, *Sparking Change to Promote Equity* reveals authors with spirit and inspiration, emotionally moved by the negative realities of past social injustices, yet motivated to conceptualize and share strategies to build and maintain advanced learning environments that maximize RCELD students' opportunities to participate and thrive. The persistent and pervasive absence of RCELD students is still prevalent in gifted and advanced education.

Social injustices in our general society are frequently replicated in schools. Microcosms of general society, schools are institutions where students and employees bring in attitudes of the general society. Schools, however, have to transcend the negative behaviors and actions occurring in the general society. Schools must develop equity goals and be able to implement them in a manner that is right, fair and just for each student. Each student attends school with expectations to be successful in a positive heterogeneous social learning environment. An excellent way to reach those goals is through guidance from empowered leaders and other educational stakeholders responsible for building more equitable and inclusive environments for diverse student populations. Here again are reasons this publication is extremely critical. It focuses on students gaining access to and actively participating in appropriate learning environments conceived and implemented by effective leaders who are prepared and ready to practice culturally responsive leadership.

I strongly encourage anyone who access this publication whether you are a veteran educational leader or someone new to educational leadership with interests in becoming a culturally responsive leader, to emulate the passionate behaviors of Dr. Roberson and Dr. Collins – choose to encourage and empower leaders to be the best they can be in building a more equitable and diverse student population within gifted and advanced programs.

Additionally, emulating their passions will translate into valuable student lessons, learnings, behaviors and actions toward equity, diversity, inclusiveness and anti-racism that will endure beyond their school days, helping them to build and participate in an even more equitable, just, righteous and inclusive future society.

Sparking Change to Promote Equity encourages all stakeholders who may not possess the courage, will, conscience or need to assume the moral responsibility to practice culturally responsive leadership for gifted and advanced programs, and take responsibility for building equity across the board so each student and staff member will benefit.

The idea of building support and enhancing equity within gifted student populations, particularly among racially, culturally, ethnically and linguistically different (RCELD) students, is not something new – the discussions have emerged through numerous significant publications and formal presentations with local, state and national forums. Overall, our discussions have focused on the root issues of educational equity, diversity, inclusiveness and anti-racism. There have been numerous successful outcomes resulting from our discussions. Two of them include the umbrella topics of culturally responsive professional learning for teachers to provide effective culturally relevant teaching and learning for students. Meaning, practical and pragmatic strategies for teachers to use in their classrooms have emerged. But why do we continue to be challenged by equity issues related to addressing the needs of RCELD students? Why are we not there yet? Why were the authors compelled to write this book on promoting equity regarding culturally responsive leadership practices in gifted and advanced programs? Complementing and adding to the existing body of work, Roberson and Collins have eloquently synthesized and succinctly focus on critical issues and importance of abilities, behaviors and efforts to incorporate culturally responsive leadership practices in gifted and advanced programs from top down.

Additionally, their added discussions have generated new excitement, envisioning an effective thought leadership for district level administrators towards effective policies for equity, diversity, inclusiveness and anti-racism school governance. New and different levels of excitement have also emerged about differences and how we can better approach them in terms of each child's background.

From my perspective as an educational administrator for over three decades for GATE and advanced level programs, *Sparking Change to Promote Equity* serves to help all educators further enhance their knowledge, skills, ability and experiences about equity. Administrators that care about equity are advancing responsible for culturally responsive leadership, recognizing that each student has different circumstances and cultural capital they bring to the learning environment. In that regard, the culturally responsive leader provides necessary resources, guidance and professional development opportunities required to assist teachers with shared aims to create equalized opportunities and outcomes for each student through established and measureable equitable practices.

It also serves to help educational leaders engage and appreciate the communities in which they serve with cultural respect and responsiveness, resisting the notion to whitewash presentation of academic subjects via cultural omissions, misrepresenting exaggerations, and distortions concerning the ancestral truths about RCELD students, particularly historically marginalized communities.

Effective Schools Movement Champion, Dr. Ron Edmonds stated:

> *"We can, whenever and wherever we choose,*
> *successfully teach all children*
> *whose schooling is of interest to us."*

For me, Dr. Edmonds' quote reflects a matter of *moral* responsibility and differentiated meaning between one size fit all educational institutions and culturally responsive and student-centered teaching approach. Taken one step further to replace 'all' with 'each' denotes individualized responsiveness. *All* refers to the entire group as a whole, while 'each' refers to the individual members of that whole group, placing a higher priority, a greater attitude and expectation on the very important differences in students. This is applicable to effective culturally responsive leaders and the staff under their watch. Their daily decisions drive their behaviors and actions.

The award-winning expertise of the Dr. Roberson and Dr. Collins qualify them to offer guidance for low and high-stakes decision making, and they are to be commended for their vision for filling existing gaps in our quest for culturally responsible leadership in gifted and advanced programs. Let each and every one of us, on our culturally responsive gifted education journey, commit to provide each and every student, including the RCELD student, appropriate rigor, challenge and supports that allow them to flourish academically, and/or to put them on a successful trajectory for college, community and career achievement.

—*Ken Dickson*

Introduction

The priorities surrounding gifted and advanced level leadership has been a topic of discussion for decades (Brown & Rinko Gay, 2017; Roberson, 2020; Michael-Chadwell, 2011; Robinson, 2021). There is continued underrepresentation in racial, cultural, ethnic, linguistic and economically different (RCELD) students in gifted and advanced programs. As classrooms continue to evolve, educators and stakeholders alike must evolve with their practices. As diversity increases among student representation, so must traditional leadership behaviors with the population it serves to be most beneficial for gifted students' academic support and success. As Black women who are also underrepresented as leaders and experts in the field of gifted and advanced learning, we present this work as a call to action for leaders to be equitable in their behaviors and to understand that special programs like gifted and talented education need leaders who value student voices, honor families and are committed to academic excellence through meaningful experience beyond content and grade-based standards.

We also want to stress that equity is a journey taken with other stakeholders. We wrote this book because we feel there is a lingering gap between research-based knowledge and practical implementation in leadership behaviors for gifted and advanced programs necessary to manifest positive, tangible, and equitable results. It is necessary in all facets of gifted and advanced level leadership. It is our hope that this book shifts the mindset and practices of gifted educators and leadership teams to prioritize the multifaceted view that cultural responsiveness is a critical component in maintaining a quality gifted education for all students. Rigor and cultural responsiveness are possible. Both are doable. However, both are not currently occuring in our schools and gifted and advanced programs. Our marginalized gifted students' cultural strengths and voices are unseen, unheard and left at the wayside untapped and underdeveloped. However, there is hope. Every educational leader can become an equitable and culturally responsive gifted leader (CRGL) regardless of background or circumstance. Although this work can be complicated, challenging and sometimes uncomfortable, it is still doable, and still necessary. It is also rewarding. Our students deserve this type of advocacy and leadership. And the paradigm shift can be achieved for those committed to the cause of equity for each gifted learner.

Framed for shared understanding, *Sparking Change to Promote Equity: Implementing Culturally Responsive Leadership Practices in Gifted and Advanced Programs* distinguishes between culturally relevant, culturally responsiveness and cultural sustainability. For the purpose of this book we describe 'culturally relevant' as relevant material and/or information that is presented with culture as a foundation for sharing, teaching and learning. Further, 'culturally responsive' indicates a process for evaluation and appropriate response to learners in a culturally appropriate manner; it is a way of communicating and messaging that recognizes the importance of including a cultural context, or cultural relevance, in all aspects of information gathering and dissemination (e.g., knowledge, experience, performance styles, etc.) for the purpose of making information encounters more relevant and effective for racially, culturally, ethnically and linguistically different (RCELD) students. In regards to culturally sustaining practice, the focus is to determine if the culturally responsive and relevant practices implemented over time has been identified as a true process to continuity and engrained within the DNA of the gifted and advanced program. The terms gifted education, gifted and advanced learning, gifted and talented (GT) education, STEM education and the like are all used interchangeably to describe advanced academics designed for students who demonstrate potential and/or have been identified as needing additional enrichment and/or accelerated service to meet their academic and skill development needs.

Sparking Change to Promote Equity begins with background information that explains why equitable leadership practices are important in schools and programs. A call to action is presented at the beginning of the book to guide the reader in review for reflection for immediate change and adaptation of policy, practices and educator preparation in advanced academics and gifted education. A call to evaluate and change leadership roles in gifted and advanced level programs offers a transition into Chapter 2, which clarifies the equity and culturally responsive lens in which this book is written. The stakeholders situated within a systemic effort for change involved, known as 'the equity train,' supports those on the journey through equitable practices in gifted and advanced programming. Chapter 3 offers information for laying the foundation of successful culturally responsive professional learning experiences for gifted teachers and leaders, promoting solutions to complex issues surrounding equitable professional learning for advanced students. A view of the various levels of gifted leadership and how professional learning input is affected is included. This is followed by a discussion of the importance of program alignment in Chapter 4, outlining the importance of designing culturally responsive gifted curriculum and instruction while bridging the connection of home and school life for students. Gifted leaders seeking to become more equitable will learn about the value a culturally responsive environment will bring to learning. In Chapter 5, we address the acultural myth—the belief that something or someone lacks culture and/or cultural influence—and its influence on current policies and practices in gifted and advanced learning. We also discuss how mining the data leads to alleviating and eliminating inequities in gifted and advanced programs. Finally, Chapter 6 reiterates the value and power of partnerships. Gifted and advanced programs cannot thrive without inclusive family and community considerations and engagement. They are essential for gifted students to thrive and for gifted leaders to flourish. Further, through co-owned colloboration, the culturally responsive gifted leader can create the conditions necessary for each student to matriculate successfully in gifted and advanced programs, and make meaning toward their own journey that is grounded with cultural capital, cultural value and personal interests.

It is important to note that *Sparking Change to Promote Equity* also takes into account harm and harm reduction—no student should be disadvantaged by content that is insensitive or disrespectful to their cultural identity; culturally responsive educators take great care not to victimize their students–encouraging a perspective that positions marginalized RCELD students as the source for their marginalization.

It is our hope that any reader of this book feels the commitment, passion and love we have for supporting equitable leadership in advanced level learning. We know this is a feat not done alone. We also know there is no "quick fix" leadership practice to address ALL the inequitable structures in education. A true decolonzing of gifted and advanced learning requires work, input and a paradigm shift examining all facets of its legacy. This is why we need equitable leaders in the field. . We must take into account the work needed beyond the scope of traditional gifted leadership. The leadership that can bring a spark of hope, positivity and one that is socially just for the betterment of our programs, students and advanced learning community.

Dr. Javetta Jones Roberson
Dr. Kristina Henry Collins

1

The Changing Tide

A Call to Action for Equitable Leadership Practices in US Schools and Programs

How can we reform education without understanding the realities of the people that we serve?

-Dr. Muhammad Khalifa

Dr. Muhammad Khalifa challenges educational leaders to simultaneously address an introspective and prospective view of equity in the provision of education to a diverse society. The field of education requires its leaders and stakeholders to consider the characteristics, experiences and needs of the children and families it serves. In order to make education equitable, purposeful and beneficial to all, educators are challenged first to understand the diversity of the lived experiences of the students in the classrooms across our nation and beyond. Educational leaders have a continuous responsibility to integrate students' personal experiences and cultures into instruction, fostering a richer learning environment for everyone. A critical self-awareness of the students' experiences is required and must involve understanding various racial and cultural backgrounds, connecting with students and within community contexts and fostering conversations on issues that affect students and families. The conversations must engage leaders in a dynamic dialogue about students' beliefs, day-to-day battles with self, racial and cultural identities,

DOI: 10.4324/9781003374923-1

and in some contexts, the challenges faced as a result of racist practices and behaviors. Each thread is critical to demonstrating how each student is valued, but also in identifying systemic issues that have been woven into the fabric of their daily lives.

Added to the conversations surrounding equity issues in education are the experiences of marginalized students as evidenced by their gross underrepresentation in gifted and advanced level programs. Nationally, less than 4% of Black students and less than 5% of Hispanic students are identified as gifted as compared to nearly 9% of White, and almost 13% of Asian students (Gentry et al., 2022). The College Board's 2022 Advanced Placment (AP) cohort report (2022) for the class of 2021 revealed a difference in test-taker proportions by race/ethnicity. Black students comprised 8.1% of all exam takers, but just 4.6% of those scoring 3 or higher. Hispanic/Latinx students, who were 25.7% of test-takers, achieved scores at a 23.6% (The College Board, 2022). Likewise, in Dual Enrollment (DE) programs, Black and Hispanic/Latinx students also have lower participation, with only 4.7% of Black students and 5.7% of Hispanic/Latinx students participating, compared to the overall participation rate of 8.1% (Fink, 2018). Systemic exclusionary practices that deny access to minoritized students for gifted and advanced level programs heed the call to action and require a significant *'leadershift'*, or shift in leadership, in schools and districts to ensure access and equity for all students. Addressing this shift will require leaders to advocate with action that challenges the status quo, engage in critical and honest discourse to dismantle systemic, oppressive structures and refute educational environments that prolong deficit views of minoritized students. Leaders must strive to understand and embrace the realities faced by students, then engage in the required transformative leadership shift to support an everchanging society of 21st century learners. The tide in education is changing and requires all educators and leaders to recognize, accept and actively address their individual roles in providing an equitable educational experience to every child and family.

The quote serves yet another purpose as a frame of reference and reminder of our (the authors') personal and collaborative career trajectories and purpose in education, specifically in

gifted and advanced education leadership. This chapter represents a call to action for educators and leaders everywhere, especially for those who lead gifted and advanced level programs. As
Black women educators and leaders in advanced level education,
we firmly believe that educational leaders must demonstrate a
positive shift in pedagogy, policy and practice to appropriately
support diverse populations and to ensure the academic success
of all students. Although great focus has been placed on instructional support for teachers, we believe the focus on significant
equitable changes in the experiences of gifted and advanced students relies heavily on the roles of school and district leaders.
To date, the actions, practices and responsibilities of leaders in
gifted and advanced learning programs along with a focus on
equity and cultural responsiveness have not been a widely discussed topic. The purpose of this book is to begin and extend
the discussions around culturally responsive gifted leadership
practices with a pristine focus on equity, inclusivity, diversity,
and belonging.

We believe it is critically important to support educational
leaders in their journey toward equitable leadership in order
for them to recognize that their leadership practices have great
impact and purpose, and to serve as a gateway for change, opportunity and access to more equitable gifted and advanced programming for racial, cultural, ethnic and linguistically different
(RCELD) students. In this context, we also include economically
disadvantaged students as they to, have been historically underrepresented in gifted and advanced programs. What we do not
want to do is to automatically "lump in" RCELD students with
being economically disadvantaged as this creates a blanketed
statement or assumption that minoritized students are always
economically disadvantaged. Although there may be some intersectionality within these student populations, we don't want to
perpetuate a stereotype of minoritized students. We also use the
term "different" instead of "diverse" in this context – to signify
those that have been historically discriminated against based on
that category not being accepted as part of the standard and/
or dominant culture – thus different in comparison to standard
or dominant euro-centric culture. It also signifies that we as a

society appreciate diversity, but it has marginalized those that are vastly different from the "colorblind" status quo and/or dominant culture. Gifted and advanced leaders must confront their personal role in the important work toward equity as it is vital to cultivating the multitude of gifts and abilities of (RCELD) students in schools everywhere.

Society's current political climate has created a false sense of hysteria around issues of diversity, equity, inclusion and social justice which has seeped into the field of gifted and advanced education, causing many stakeholders to feel any efforts to this end challenge the fragility of individuals whose primary goal is to keep systemic inequity at the forefront of programs and services. As a result, so-called 'allies' paint the picture of a watered-down foundation of cultural responsiveness and equity in gifted and advanced education. Herein lies the beauty of this book: our personal, lived experiences as Black students, educators, leaders and mothers uniquely poise us to tell our stories in each respective role with poignant revelation and clarity. Our goal is to help you navigate your journey into culturally responsive, equitable leadership while standing firm in our commitment fidelity to being culturally responsive leaders in gifted and advanced education. You will be able to engage in critical dialogue with action to follow with your colleagues on best practices in culturally responsive gifted leadership for your school, program and district, moving to eliminate barriers which will ultimately positively impact future generations of both teachers and students.

Evolution of Equity in Education

Inequality and inequity are no strangers to education. For centuries, subpar and unequal access to quality education, services, educators, resources and facilities have plagued African American students. Added to this group over recent years is the multitude of Latinx students who have entered American schools yearning for fair and equitable access to education. Far too many marginalized students to count have been on the receiving end of unjust educational experiences.

A cornerstone of the civil rights movement, the landmark Supreme Court case Brown v. Board of Education, established that 'separate-but-equal' education was not only unconstitutional but more poignantly, not at all equal. Prior to the pivotal case, access to quality education for African Americans was barred, punitive and dismissive (Davis, 2021). To that end, and in a similar fashion, the origin of gifted education was similarly poised, denying identification, placement and access to gifted education programming to persons of color. For too many decades to count, access to gifted education programs has been somewhat of a mirage for RCELD students seen but faintly, not clearly and almost as if not there or accessible at all.

Education reform has been a hot topic of discussion over the past several decades, resulting in several changes in urban, rural, inner city and suburban classrooms. Interspersed in the discussions are fiscal challenges to providing quality educational experiences for all children, educator preparation and professional learning needs, teacher and student demographics and the increasing diversity of student populations. The academic, social and emotional needs of our gifted and advanced youth must be addressed with equity at the forefront to ensure that the unique needs of all students are appropriately met within the context of systemic reform efforts.

Common within educational settings is the tendency for people to befuddle the terms *equity* and *equality*. Equality represents fairness and the same, equal treatment for all students. Equity recognizes the unique experiences of individuals and focuses on fairness-based on individual difference or need. In many school settings, educators serve a multitude of student populations from varying backgrounds and experiences; therefore the impetus for demonstrated, equitable leadership is paramount. In theory and a perfectly equal society, equity and equality would share a definition; however, inequalities in the real world make it necessary to differentiate between the two. Simply put, you cannot have true equality in education without interweaving equity when and where needed in just the right amount for each student. This can only be achieved by knowing, accepting and nurturing each student according to what his or her true needs, challenges and abilities are.

Equity in education is realized when every student receives the appropriate resources needed to acquire the basic skills to reach their respective optimal level. In order for educators to provide educational equity for each student, school and district leaders must ensure there are not any barriers to students' ability to achieve their optimal potential. Further, students' personal and social circumstances must not impede their success. In an equitable educational setting, deficit ideologies that focus on classism and racism and which lead to discriminatory, oppressive practices are dismissed and barred. Discrimination of any kind, based on socioeconomic, racial, gender, cultural or other factors is not allowed. In an equitable educational setting, each student receives the basic minimum standard, the right to an appropriate education, and specific attention to individual needs, regardless of the additional support that may be required. In sum, equitable education is individual in nature, meeting each student's needs while simultaneously meeting the collective needs of all students.

Equity issues continue to challenge gifted and advanced programs in schools and districts across the US and globally. The nominations and referrals of students from underrepresented populations such as Black, Latinx and Native Americans for gifted programs and exclusionary programs, policy and retention efforts continue to create a persistent gap in the representation of these students. This gap also goes for courses aligned to Advanced Academics such as Advanced Placement (AP) course and Dual Enrollment (DE) pathways as they too, historically have experienced underrepresentation of marginalized students (Fink, 2018; Yang & Gentry, 2023; Roberson, 2020; Whiting & Ford, 2009). As the issues become more complex, the need for leadership practices that have the capability to transform educational outcomes for racial, cultural, ethnic economic and linguistically different (RCELD) students continues to grow.

True educational equity requires the expertise of engaged leaders, stakeholders and supporters. Across schools and districts, leadership roles should be filled with key decision makers who can shift policies and procedures, and demonstrate progressive leadership and systemic change in overall academic achievement and access to equitable programming for all students.

The Changing Tide

Racial and ethnic distributions of public school students across the country have shifted and school demographics are increasingly diverse as an influx of students from traditionally non-English speaking backgrounds have entered schools and districts across the US. The increase in the number of students who are non-traditional speaking English students within the past decade requires a shift in how educators teach and lead in elementary and secondary school settings (Roberson & Floyd, 2020). Nationally, Hispanic/Latinx student enrollment multiplied from 2009 to 2020, and the percentage of Hispanic/Latinx public school students increased from 22% to 28% (USDOE, 2021). Although the racial and ethnic composition of public schools varies from state to state, between 2009 and 2020, the percentage of White public school students was lower in 2020 than in 2009 in all states. Enrollment of White public school students will continue to decline, and NCES (2022) projected that in 2029, White students will make up 43.8% of public school enrollment compared to 64.8% in 1995, and 49.5% in 2014, respectively. Further NCES projections indicated a continued increase between 2020 and 2030 in the percentage of Hispanic students enrolled in US schools.

As diverse student populations continue to increase, so does the need for more appropriate and specialized programs to serve them within schools. Notable academic programs such as Advanced Placement (AP), Gifted and Dual Enrollment (DE) are all experiencing a surge in student diversity. Although an increase in diversity in advanced programs is noted, disparities in the representation of minoritized students therein remains (Roberson, 2020; The College Board, 2014). In many states, these programs fall under college and career readiness indicators for success and are included in state accountability ratings. The access and opportunity gaps that plague RCELD students in these programs have the potential of continuing after they graduate. Educational leaders who espouse culturally responsive practices must demonstrate equitable leadership by focusing on closing opportunity gaps while dismantling the inequitable structures that are common to these notable programs.

Reframing Equitable Leadership in Gifted and Advanced Level Programs

Increasing diversity in student demographics calls for inclusive leadership strategies and whole school and program approaches that address student marginalization issues. The strategies will require going beyond the typical surface level 'achievement' gap data discussions to addressing disparities through true leadership reform efforts. To this end, instructional leaders must enforce policies requiring educators to engage in dialogue and instructional practices that support organizational diversity and inclusion efforts (Roberson & Floyd, 2020). Culturally responsive gifted leadership practices support advanced level programs through the positive reshaping of specialized schools and programs with historically underrepresented and underserved populations when they utilize leadership behaviors that reflect the needs of the populations being served. Implementing a culturally responsive framework demonstrates best practices for educators to create inclusive learning environments that enable and empower all gifted students while exposing them to rigorous and advanced learning and engagement (Davis et al., 2021).

Culturally responsive leadership (Khalifa, 2018) stems from the work of Dr. Gloria Ladson Billings (1995) who coined the term *culturally relevant pedagogy (CRP)* and Dr. Geneva Gay's framework of *culturally responsive teaching (CRT)*. Within the CRP framework, each educator is encouraged to exhibit a healthy respect for student diversity in their classroom and school. To extend the work of Dr. Billings, culturally responsive leadership, or CRL, requires leaders to be critically self-reflective, develop and sustain culturally responsive teachers and curricula, promote inclusive and anti-oppressive school contexts and engage within the context of the communities represented in their school (Khalifa, 2018). Culturally responsive leaders are responsible for ensuring that all school and district educators are representative of the students they serve and are supportive of the culturally rich instruction they require to thrive (Roberson & Floyd, 2020). Leaders who demonstrate and promote culturally responsive practices by appropriately attending to the social, cultural and emotional needs of their diverse students must also require the same of the teachers they lead (Gay, 2010).

In the context of equitable leadership that supports gifted and advanced level programs, we've utilize the aforementioned foundational tents of Khalifa's Culturally Responsive Leadership along with the 5 abilities of Equity Literacy (Gorski and Swalwell, 2023). Those abilities include being able to recognizing inequity, respond to the inequity recognized, redressing inequity in an active manner, cultivating equity to further its cause and sustain equity. Collectively, we adapted traditional gifted and advanced level leadership practices to develop a framework for Culturally Responsive Gifted Leadership. Viewed from a standpoint of critical reflectivity for leaders in gifted and advanced education, Culturally Responsive Gifted Leadership (CRGL) can serve as a catalyst for a paradigm shift of traditional leadership within advanced education. Culturally responsive gifted leaders promote positive change, eliminating deficit-thinking and oppressive structures for minoritized students and critically reflect on their leadership practice as a continuous improvement measure (Roberson, 2023).

What we offer in supporting you as a new, or seasoned, equity leader in gifted education has the potential to permanently change the trajectory of a child's life. In this text, we will break down concepts and utilize critical language that gifted and advanced leaders must learn for RCELD students to flourish. We will address the 'traditional" elephant' in the room regarding the politics, systemic practices and pedagogical needs inherent in gifted and advanced education while supporting leaders in finding balance and setting priorities to benefit their students and programs. Although there are structural and historical inequities that have plagued the field of gifted and advanced education for decades, and certainly long before we came into this profession, our goal is to personally assist you in navigating the need to promote equity in leadership spaces and put practices in place to transform, and not perpetuate, inequity in the field.

As you engage in this text and reflect on the complexities of today's schools and advanced programs, it is our hope that you personally apply the following tenets and concepts to frame your future dialogue with others and practices in your respective area to solidify an equitable, culturally responsive gifted leadership framework. We encourage you:

1) *Remain open to a paradigm shift:* In order to truly incorporate cultural responsiveness and equity as a leader in gifted and advanced education, you must be willing to open your mind to change and shift your current thought processes. A paradigm shift is vital to your growth as an equitable leader.

2) *Discuss, collaborate, and critically self-reflect with others in gifted and advanced education:* While the projected outcome from this text is to learn and grow as an equitable leader, we want you to reflect on your own practices and be open to discussions and collaborations with others throughout the process.

3) *Serve as a change agent:* Some of your colleagues will find value in the equity work while others may not. By collaborating with other like-minded individuals, you can expand the equity knowledge base and build trust among your colleagues. Throughout your equity work, be encouraged to empower educators at all levels—teachers, principals, teacher leaders, coordinators and district leaders to develop solutions to inequities in gifted education.

4) *Be transparent and honest about the journey along the way:* No one wins when we are not honest with ourselves about the journey to equity. As a leader, it is possible you may experience vulnerability, discomfort or engage in difficult conversations when applying our framework. All of these represent healthy engagement in the work and are needed to achieve success. As you express your authentic self throughout this journey to become a culturally responsive gifted leader healthy, open and honest dialogue is required.

Remember, critical, and even difficult, conversations have the ability to lead to positive outcomes.

5) ***Rise like a phoenix***: Although you may experience vulnerability and difficulty during your equitable leadership journey, remember not to remain in those spaces. Determine your intentions, set personal goals and remember to trust the process. We want you to feel a sense of urgency in putting in place the action steps for an equitable gifted and advanced education program. Establish a solid framework to create growth opportunities for you, your staff and students. In this way, the challenges faced will not prevail and the successful strategies you have put into practice will ensure your experiences and the program will rise like a phoenix and soar to greater heights!

Our techniques have proven successful for us and many of our colleagues across the US and globally. We are excited to share our strategies with you, foster your personal and professional growth and assist you as you become a culturally responsive gifted leader.

Questions to Critically Self-reflect on Your Journey

Included in our efforts to reform gifted and advanced program leaders and educators and to support your growing identity as a gifted leader who is embarking on an equitable leadership journey, we have developed a series of questions for in-depth analysis and critical self-reflection to engage in the following chapters. Being critical and self-reflective as a leader ensures you have an awareness of your current practices and how they can provide opportunities for growth. Being critically self-reflective builds a continuous improvement mindset. This also presents leaders with an opportunity to come to grips with any biases, prejudices and assumptions they may unknowingly have as a leader. From curriculum and instructional support to community building, to assessments selected and implemented, these all play a part in leaders appropriately accessing and mining program data.

The following questions are shared here to spark your reflection on equitable leadership practices within the school or organization for which you are a stakeholder:

1. What represents your 'changing tide' as an educational leader? What has prompted you to begin the process of initiating equitable change in your gifted program?
2. Will having a solid knowledge of the historical inequities in education (including gifted and advanced education) affect your current and future equity-based work? Why or why not?
3. What are three (3) goals or perspectives you would like to achieve after reading this book?
4. How can you support other leaders and stakeholders with engaging in culturally responsive or equity-based work?

2

Begin with Equity in Mind

Gifted and Advanced Academics through a Culturally Responsive Leadership Lens

Equity can never become a reality in education if it is viewed as charity instead of a professional obligation.

-Dr. Anthony Muhhamad

As leaders in gifted and advanced education, we must ensure that our view and responsibility for equity is responsively centered on the holistic needs of the students, effective training of teachers and authentic inclusion of stakeholders. Equity should never be viewed as a compliance checklist, MTSS strategy or 'after-market' curriculum tool. It should not be expressed as a limited consideration such as: 'Well, I was equitable for today' or 'I was culturally responsive for this...we are good here.' We must make sure our efforts within equity are genuine. Equity must be embedded in everyday practices and woven into the fabric of our gifted programs. Ingrained in our program's DNA, it becomes who we 'are' versus something we 'do.'

As you embark on this journey of culturally responsive gifted leadership, equity will be at the forefront and evident in the behaviors you exhibit. From decision making to policy implementation to family and community connectivity, you will be equipped to lead the 'equity train' in your gifted program. But how does that look? Who is all on the equity train? How do I

DOI: 10.4324/9781003374923-2

incorporate equity into gifted and advanced level programs? And what is my role as an advanced level leader striving to be more equitable? Let's take an in-depth look at these questions to start you on your new journey.

Envisioning Equity-based Leadership Practices in Gifted Education

How do you, as a gifted and advanced leader, ensure that your leadership behaviors are equitable? In Chapter 1, we discussed equity in education-fairness based on individual differences and the need to ensure that each child receives what they need in order to have a successful educational experience. In recent years, considerable attention has been placed on equity in educational settings due to an abundant increase in RCELD student populations in schools and programs including gifted and advanced placement. Because of this increase, there is a need for leaders to be equipped with certain tools and strategies to effectively serve RCELD students with fidelity. To achieve equity in gifted education, leaders must commit to serving each and every student in a way that is fair, accommodating, inclusive and anti-oppressive. Leaders in gifted education must make a deliberate effort to steer away from perpetuating the negative remnants of earlier conceived notions of giftedness where intelligence was defined and normed by a euro-centric, white dominant perspective. Equitable leadership in gifted and advanced programs should place a valiant effort into intentionally shifting their approach to serve students in gifted and advanced education that reflect a responsive environment designed to maximize potential and the cultural capital in each student.

The Equity Train

Who all is on the 'equity train' in gifted and advanced education? The "equity train" is a phrase that has been used by many scholars and practitioners of various fields to convey the concept of equity in terms of fairness and justice. Dr. Joy Lawson Davis, a prominent scholar in the field of gifted and advanced education, has referred to the equity train in presentations to foster a sense of responsibilty for all stakeholders in gifted education. The train metaphor may also be used to symbolize overall movement and progress toward achieving greater equity in gifted and advanced education. Each train has an end goal and destination. Aboard that moving train is the transport of goods, services and/or people from one location to the next along its designated track. We further posit that people are not mere passengers aboard the equity train, passively awaiting arrival to the destination. It takes a group of skilled and trained people to support the train's journey to its final destination. Onboard are dedicated stakeholders committed to incorporating equitable-based practices to individually support each student in gifted education, and everyone has a role. —The gifted leader serves as the conductor, steering it to reach its destination. There are other major roles toward the train's successful journey to include engineers, onboard service crew members, customers/passengers and those that laid the track itself. Figure 2.1 illustrates an example of educational professional as major stakeholders on the equity train.

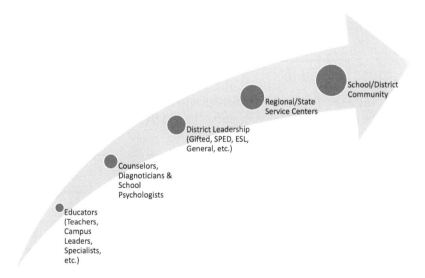

FIGURE 2.1 Key stakeholders on the equity train for gifted and advanced education.

Keeping with the train metaphor, students, their families, and broader school district's community are akin to customers/passengers with whom we collaboratively serve. Those that enact and influence the policy and curriculum, including those affiliated with regional/state service centers are akin to those who help lay the track, which ultimately controls the available route to the destination. For the equity train to be fully functional, the culturally responsive gifted leader (as the conductor) need all of the key stakeholders to help you stay on track toward your goals and the equity journey in general. As other onboard service crew members, educators and counselors directly influence and/or educate our students. The district leadership (i.e., curriculum coordinators, departmental directors and superintendents), serves as engineers, keeping the train operating at in acceptable conditions. and supports staff along the journey Because equity is a priority to you as the conductor, you must foster and promote it as a non-negotiable priority for everyone evidenced in the the approach and deliverables of their work. The equity train is a collaborative space for everyone to grow and serve for the sake of gifted students. As another point for priority, many of our gifted students are also served in other populations (special education, multilingual, etc.); therefore, it's imperative that you create a common space (train stations) to join forces with others on your journey.

CRGL Leadershift

Invite equity train members to site-based committee or district committee meetings to add their voices and perspectives.

Lastly, we cannot forget about the regional and state service centers and our school and community partnerships. The state and regional service centers are a viable resource for schools and districts as they can provide professional learning opportunities and unite efforts that give a bird's eye view of what can be done to help gifted students. They are also informative on up to date and soon-to-be legislation and accountability needs surrounding gifted and advanced learning. This in return keeps equity train members abreast of any upcoming changes or pertinent information. School and community partnerships tie into this category as those stakeholders make equity train members aware of needs in the community. We've included university and college teacher and leader preparation programs in this group as they are preparing our future gifted educators to enter the field in an equitable manner. We need them to have a critical consciousness about equitable gifted practices in the field as they connect the theory to what we practice everyday.

These individuals will make this collective effort valuable as their advocacy will be instrumental in the equity journey. A trajectory of a child's life can be positively changed forever by ensuring the intentionality of equitable practices on the journey. The people on the journey with you are vital. Keep note, equity is not a 'one-stop shop' in gifted education. We must 'grow' through it as it grows through us. We must nurture, foster and guide others as we ourselves receive guidance and mentorship. As history has taught us in education, all things evolve and grow. You, as a gifted leader, must be willing to grow and evolve on the equity journey.

What Would You Do?

Lydia was a brand new gifted campus coordinator at Ward Elementary School. Her school's student demographics were as follows: 35% Black/African American, 55% Latinx/Hispanic, 5% two or more races, 2% Asian and 3% White. Around 94% of students were on free/reduced lunch and about 18% multilingual. The school was located in a low SES neighborhood. Parent participation was low for campus events, but there were dedicated teachers that wanted to support the students and school community. As a new coordinator, Lydia asked the campus principal for the current year's enrollment data for students identified as gifted and talented at Ward. The campus principal did not have any information and suggested she speak with the district elementary coordinator. When speaking to the district coordinator and receiving information, she was shocked to find that no 3rd and 4th grade students from the previous year were identified as GT. When asked to see the nomination and referral applications from the previous year, the district coordinator expressed that the campus 'did not have any referrals or nominations.' Stunned, but eager to develop a plan for equitable nomination and identification, Lydia went on to speak to the campus principal about how she can support the campus teachers and community by nominating students, professional learning for identifying various gifted populations and creating an on campus GT committee to help build a more equitable gifted program. The principal responded, 'Well...GT really hasn't been a focus due to our accountability rating from standardized testing. I don't think this is a priority right now and honestly, I don't want to put more on teachers right now. Hiring has been rough and I need all the teachers I can get right now. Can we focus on this next year?' Lydia was devastated. She wanted to be the best coordinator but also needed cooperation and buy in from her campus administrator to move forward.

Questions:

1. How could Lydia explain/respond to her campus principal the urgency of creating a more equitable nomination, referral and professional learning for gifted people on their campus, based on the data and information received?

2. Since standardized testing is mentioned as a priority, how could Lydia connect nominations, referrals and giftedness in general to standardized test scores and accountability? Is there a need to connect the two? Why or why not?

3. What policies currently exist in your district about nomination and referrals of potential students? Are

> you provided data each year on who is currently identified as gifted on your campus? The nomination and referral data?

Integrating Culturally Responsive Leadership Practices in Advanced Level Programs

We now know who all are on the equity train as gifted and advanced leaders. Let's now focus on what leadership behaviors can best serve us on this journey. A typical or traditional leadership focusing gifted and advanced program has consisted of identification, assessments, policy, evaluation, program enrollment and curriculum/instruction to name a few. Over the years, dimensions of diversity, equity and inclusion have been slow to be addressed as a means to support a successful gifted program. The limited discourse on DEI (Diversity, Equity and Inclusion) topics, along with histories and disparities associated with them within gifted and advanced leadership, has been noticeably missing. With the increase of student diversity in public schools across the US (NCES, 2023), the need for leaders to engage in a framework designed with each gifted student in mind is much needed. We understand there is not a one size fits all approach to addressing DEI topics in gifted and advanced education. Nor do we believe that there is one leadership style that can fix the missingness of these important topics. However, we do believe that our recommendations, framework and strategies can be used to adequately address the multifaceted aspects of diversity, equity and inclusion in gifted and advanced leadership. Our strategies aim to counteract and transform- not perpetuate inequities that still continue to negatively affect the field of gifted and advanced education.

Implementing culturally responsive gifted leadership is one way to promote positive, socially just change in gifted and advanced programs. As mentioned in Chapter 1, culturally responsive leadership is characterized by a unique set of leadership behaviors that reflect and promote inclusive philosophies and policies while leaders are continuously finding ways to challenge societal inequities that have plagued education for years. Culturally responsive leaders implement change to focus on improving educational outcomes for each student, especially those who come from historically marginalized communities.

CRGL Leadershift

Civil discourse is needed between stakeholders on all things equity in gifted and advanced learning. Connect with them to understand what equity means for the gifted and advanced program and how that meaning affects accountability, social/emotional well being and family needs.

When viewing leadership behaviors needed in gifted and advanced programs, we've adapted this approach along with embedding Gorski and Swalwell's (2023) 5 abilities of Equity Literacy and traditional gifted and advanced level leadership practices to provide another way for gifted and advanced leaders to affirm their commitment to equity, diversity, social justice and inclusivity. As a culturally responsive gifted leader, you will be purposeful, fearless and intentional about every decision you make regarding your students and overall program. Your behaviors will exemplify critical self-reflection in everything you do while keeping a growth mindset for the days ahead. You will see yourself as an advocate for change in gifted and advanced education while understanding that sometimes, change can upset people—and that's okay. You will welcome discourse on racism, social justice and inequity countering the narrative of being a quiet, silent leader on these topics. You will recognize and acknowledge that at the inception of gifted and advanced level programs, the status quo was that giftedness and high potential could only be identified in students who were white. Staying abreast on the historical context of gifted and advanced learning, you will gain knowledge to understand that many researchers during this timeframe were tainted with racial prejudice in identification and assessment measures. As a result of this view, many non-white students with high potential were overlooked, unseen and not identified to be served in this capacity. Knowing that history, you will work to positively shift the narrative and eradicate inequity in your program to reflect the beautiful diversity of this world. This includes diversity in race, ethnicity, language, disability and economic status. You will be at the forefront of building capacity with your program, developing student agency and have a relentless determination to shift your program environment with equity in mind. You will challenge the status quo with action. Please note, we also apply "Culturally Responsive Gifted Leader" behaviors to programs that support advanced learning outside of gifted education such as the Advanced Placement (AP) program and Dual enrollment (DE) courses. The reasoning behind this expansion is simple. Initially, when we conceptualized these attributes and framework for leaders, we realized there was a missing link in equitable leadership behaviors over our years as leaders in gifted education. But as we matriculated through elementary, secondary and post-secondary education, we felt it was necessary to include these upper level programs as the need for equitable leadership was needed in this space as well. We wanted to highlight some integral behaviors and examples we believe contribute to being a successful culturally responsive gifted leader. Below, we provide some culturally responsive gifted leader attributes you can use to support the paradigm shift that is needed for your program holistically.

TABLE 2.1 Examples of Culturally Responsive Gifted Leader Behaviors and Impacts for Gifted/Advanced Level Programs

Traditional Gifted/ Advanced Leadership Behaviors/Focus	Culturally Responsive Gifted/Advanced Leader Behaviors/Focus	Possible Impact on Gifted/Advanced Level Program
Programming	Critical self-reflection of practices (policy, procedures, program holistically and leadership style) Change, adapt and modify based on the critical self-reflection to eliminate bias and inequity Acknowledge, recognize and conduct discourse the historical inequity of gifted and advanced programs with stakeholders	Increase school-based culturally responsive Gifted leadership protocols Require gifted program data on culturally responsive and sustaining practices (Professional learning of staff, curriculum and instruction used, policy, etc.)
Curriculum and Instruction/ Professional Learning	Developing and sustaining culturally responsive teachers and curriculum embedded within gifted and advanced program. Provide Research and Maintain professional learning opportunities that are free of bias, deficit-thinking and dated practices that target minoritized gifted and advanced students	Increase diversity of gifted and advanced program and school curricula and activities Provide and guide gifted and advanced educators with authentic examples of culturally responsive education in both theory and practice Promote and foster equitable professional learning communities for gifted and advanced level educators

(Continued)

TABLE 2.1 (Continued)

Traditional Gifted/ Advanced Leadership Behaviors/Focus	Culturally Responsive Gifted/Advanced Leader Behaviors/Focus	Possible Impact on Gifted/Advanced Level Program
Learning Environments	Promoting inclusive, anti-oppressive and Anti-Racist educational contexts in gifted and advanced education	Students and Indigenous communities are mirrored and reflected within gifted and advanced programs. within the stakeholder groups. Up to date research an equitable practices for gifted and advanced learning are incorporated in the learning environment. All realms of diversity, Equity, Inclusion and Belonging are recognized, welcomed and incorporated within the learning environment.
Learning and Development	Engaging in students' indigenous (or local) school community contexts through improved participation and representation of diverse Guardians and community stakeholders in school/program culture	Establish a partnership between the school and community by inviting stakeholders into schools, visiting gifted and advanced level programs and integrating the culture of students and community members in school/program activities

(Continued)

TABLE 2.1 (Continued)

Traditional Gifted/ Advanced Leadership Behaviors/Focus	Culturally Responsive Gifted/Advanced Leader Behaviors/Focus	Possible Impact on Gifted/Advanced Level Program
Assessments/Program Evaluation	Incorporate equitable assessments Incorporate equitable evaluation methods for gifted and advanced programs	Equity audits Culturally Responsive evaluation Equity teams

Adapted with permission.

The Blessing and Burden of being a Culturally Responsive Gifted Leader

Have you ever heard the term 'good trouble?' The incomparable John Lewis spoke these words when relating to anything that is good for social justice, equity and beyond, and for the greater good of people in general. Being a culturally responsive gifted leader may sometimes require you to get in 'good trouble.' Any work in creating systems and structures designed to dismantle disparities for underrepresented student groups will require you to develop strength mentally, physically and emotionally. Equity work like this is work of the heart and soul. It is something that is embedded in everything you say and do as a culturally responsive gifted leader. It can be tiring. It can be frustrating. You will experience roadblocks that you must come against. But the work is necessary. The work is needed. And your program will thrive because of your decision to go beyond 'what traditionally works' as a leader in gifted and advanced education.'

Questions to Critically Self-reflect on your Journey

1. Which of these behaviors of a culturally responsive gifted leader am I currently incorporating in my everyday leadership journey? Which ones do I need to focus more on? Which ones do I need to expand my learning on?

2. Who are my equity train stakeholders? How can I collaborate with them on my gifted and advanced program 'equity track and journey?'
3. How can I focus on DEI topics with my equity train stakeholders in a way that is easily understood and not meant to look like an 'extra thing' they have to do?
4. How can I critically self-reflect on past interactions with stakeholders on DEI topics for the gifted and move forward in addressing topics so they can be at the core of my gifted and advanced program and leadership focus?

3

Building From the Ground Up

Laying the Foundation Through Culturally Responsive Professional Learning

Students with high academic ability benefit when educators are trained in gifted education pedagogy and therefore better prepared to meet students' advanced needs.

-Brigandi et al., 2018

Oftentimes, the debate over core issues related to students' and/or early career professionals' preparation and performance—or lack thereof—results in a circular and bi-directional blame game whereby industry blames universities; universities and other post-secondary institutions blame secondary schools; secondary schools blame elementary schools; elementary schools blame families and/or the student's background; and families blame the government and/or industry for the current state of inequalities, opportunity and so on—and vice versa. The biggest fallacy in this debate is a central mindset that there exists this fictitious, institutionalized 'culturally irresponsible beast' that we are all fighting against, and ignoring the more plausible reality that collective irresponsive practices of [un]trained individuals at each of these levels create the issues at hand. In this chapter, we want to highlight and create an awareness of a) practical and culturally responsive influence for students, b) culturally responsive professional learning in teachers' training and c) ostensible solutions

DOI: 10.4324/9781003374923-3

to a complex and lingering education problem of student performance—more specifically in gifted education—maximizing students' potential for optimum performance and achievement.

Within each of the aforementioned critical sources of influence in any student educational trajectory are those who have the responsibility to educate the student. This educational process is not 'acultural' (Collins, 2021). Educators equip students with the tools that accelerate their learning, engagement, innovation and the sense of discovery they need to excel in a 21st century workforce and in their academic lives. Culturally responsive gifted educators at early childhood, elementary and secondary levels of schooling understand this educational trajectory plan that students' matriculate through from pre-kindergarten to 12th grade

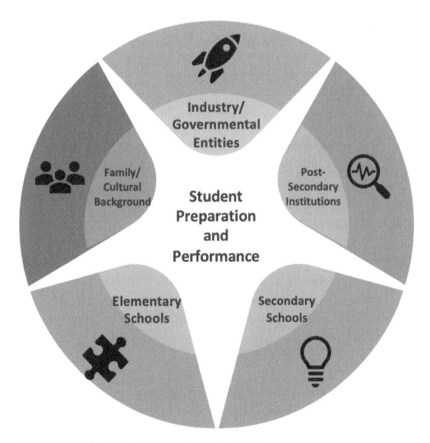

FIGURE 3.1 Critical cultural influences in student development.

and beyond has major impact on the rest of the students' lives. Core and elective content such as Career and Technical Education (CTE) and Fine Arts, are also a part of student trajectory at the middle and high school levels. Culturally responsive gifted educators align their professional preparation and learning towards these influences for student development. They collaborate with students and their families in enriching the learning experience, incorporating student background for value meaning-making purposes. Connecting with post-secondary institutions and governmental industries allows gifted educators to stay current on research-based promising practices and industry needs and prepare students for the workforce or the career field they are interested in. Culturally responsive gifted educators are intentional in enhancing influences for student development as they see beyond their current circumstances, creating a pathway to help students prepare for their own future.

CRGL Leadershift

Design and deliver professional learning that is and promotes culturally responsive inclusion and consideration of all voices (stakeholders).

Levels of Leadership in Gifted Education

When referring to gifted educators in this text, we are focusing on any stakeholder that supports advanced level programming in schools. This term also includes leaders in gifted education. Leadership, used in the broadest term, refers to anyone who is in a position to cast and/or lead the vision for any organization. Within gifted education, that leadership includes beginning and advanced gifted education professionals (BAGEP; see national gifted educator standards, https://nagc.org/page/National -Standards-in-Gifted-and-Talented-Education). BAGEPs include teachers new to the teaching profession as well as experienced educator professionals new to teaching within gifted programs. Advanced gifted educational professionals include those in teacher leader roles and/or those who facilitate the professional learning of others (i.e., gifted coordinators, curriculum developers, assistant principals, principals and administrative evaluators). School district directors of advanced academics, assistant superintendents of curriculum and instruction and other administrative positions are also included in this definition, depending on how they are connected to gifted education within the school system's or program's organizational structure. Educators and leaders of the gifted should progress toward development and growth as they progress through time in service and their professional roles.

Laying the Foundation for Culturally Responsive Professional Learning

Leaders and facilitators of professional learning in gifted education must first distinguish between a) culture-blind principles disguised as neutral-based skill development that approach giftedness, learning [dis]abilities and skill-based training from a perceived 'cultural' perspective that victimizes RCELD students and b) culturally responsive talent development, which integrates principles of cognitive diversity and cultural capital within responsive identity development and skills training processes (Collins, 2021; see also Cotton et al., 2022; Collins, 2018; Grantham et al., 2020), and eliminate the former Culturally responsive professional learning (CRPL) for gifted educators must be grounded in non-exclusionary practices for maximum student success. CRPL provides an array of learning opportunities focused on the most up to date research to increase the knowledge base for gifted educators in their program.

CRPL, as a cultural-sustaining tool, is grounded in a strength-based equity lens and identity development (Collins, 2018). As illustrated in Figure 3.2, we introduce CRPL that is uniquely positioned at the intersectionality of multicultural gifted education (MCGE; Ford, 2011), educator professional development and mentoring across the lifespan (Collins, 2016).

FIGURE 3.2 Foundation for culturally responsive professional learning in gifted education.

Ford (2011) introduced the concept of multicultural gifted education (MGCE), characterized by the multiple pathways in which educators develop curriculum that will affect students culturally and cognitively. The MCGE approach increases rigor and utilizes the gifted student's interest while infusing higher level cultural content with higher order thinking skill development, leading to positive student self-concept and student academic outcomes. Educator professional development, as a component of professional learning, is framed by identity and talent development models (Varelas et al., 2013; Collins, 2018) to ensure both professional growth for the educator and academic growth for their students while keeping up with the latest developments in the scholarship of teaching and learning (SoTL). Mentoring has been identified and echoed many times over as a key factor underlying success by individuals at any stage in life. Effective mentorship begins with a discovery of one's own philosophy, methods and style of mentoring. The process of developing an effective method of mentoring takes years; it must be continually adjusted and redirected to meet the objective and needs of students. Culturally responsive mentoring (CRM; Byers-Winston, 2014) includes recognition of development of one's own multicultural self and how it influences what is valued and prioritized, and an awareness of the ways that cultural factors impact relationships, teaching and learning. As a cultural-sustaining tool, mentoring across the career lifespan of an educator establishes a multifaculty, research-based, vertical mentoring approach that is interdisciplinary, multifaceted and responsive (Collins, 2016) to the challenges of scholarly development and sustained faculty persistence. It directly impacts educational institution capacity. Together, these three concepts lay a foundation for a culturally responsive professional learning model that engenders a profound sense of confidence and responsibility in all gifted stakeholders to be culturally responsive, and to incorporate responsiveness at all levels in systemic ways—defeating the fictitious, institutionalized 'culturally irresponsible beast.' With this foundation, beginner and advanced gifted education professionals are more likely to replicate, implement and maintain the principles and practices learned in a CRPL.

As shown in Figure 3.2, at the intersection of these, CRPL extends the principles of an effective cognitive and professional development into a foundation for a) increased and sustained productivity of career faculty and b) a culturally responsive support system and pathway for faculty to thrive and dynamically develop. Guided by participatory and action-based research and intervention, CRPL also addresses the following leadership components that we recommend for any advanced learning program:

◆ Development and use of validation measures to evaluate effective and sustainable culturally responsive professional learning.
◆ Positive cultivation of the organic, and sometimes informal, undercurrent and system of supports and connectedness among faculty.
◆ Examination of the practices for educator recruitment and retention that impact student performance and achievement.

◆ Consistent evaluation of the conditions under which professional learning is conducted, and the factors that promote or inhibit effective development and implementation of a more inclusive curriculum.

This three-pronged CRPL model features components that are substantially stronger and more equitable when integrated together. It offers an effective solution and distinctive progression toward culturally sustainable talent development of faculty within a nested system of supports that positively impacts gifted students' identity, academic preparation and performance.

What Would You Do?

Kelsey is a new district coordinator who wants to provide more professional learning opportunities for her gifted teachers. Kelsey works in a school district that serves about 10,000 students, K–12th grade. She supports all grade levels of gifted students and teachers. She really wants to create multiple opportunities for her teachers to be trained on the following: social/emotional needs of the gifted, identification and assessment, differentiation, and depth and complexity. Her available funding has limited. Her gifted teachers have expressed a need to get more foundational, professional learning related to gifted and advanced education. Kelsey wants to offer a book study, collaborate with the local regional service centers and offer professional learning during the summer months. However, she is struggling with how to organize the events with building principals and district-leveladministrators. She is doing everything by herself and this is her second year in the gifted coordinator role. Kelsey feels overwhelmed.

1. *What other partnerships or collaboration opportunities could Kelsey seek to help with the professional learning of her gifted teachers?*
2. *What are some organizational resources that could help Kelsey to structure year-long professional learning that is meaningful for her teachers?*

3. *How can Kelsey get support and connect with campus- and district-level leadership to coordinate three-pronged culturally responsive professional learning that is appropriate for (gifted and advanced program'ming at each of the districts educational levels?*

Setting Campus- and District-level Goals

Goal setting by is an essential process inwhen incorporating our three-pronged culturally responsive professional learning (CRPL) model for gifted and advanced educators. Educational goals arecommon attributes for measuring the improvement or progression of an initiative or objective. Although there are many strategies that support specific goal settings in schools and programs, we aver that the SMARTIE goals framework best serves and fosters equity-based outcomes. SMARTIE goals are specific, measurable, attainable, relevant (or realistic and results-focused), timely, inclusive and equitable (The Management Center, 2021). They are inherently more likely to yield positive and tangible results for responsive improvement within professional learning. SMARTIE goals support scope and sequence for desired equitable student outcomes and create timelines that are aligned to the compacted nature of gifted and advanced level programming. Because SMARTIE goals are not equity-neutral, they foster a shift from a restricted one size fits all model into powerful model of connectedness amongst stakeholders at all levels to include considerations and priorities for individual student success.

Sustained, in-depth CRPL offers educators an opportunity to constantly learn new strategies, translate and implement new knowledge into practice, reflect and gather feedback and responsively modify instruction (Novak & Lewis, 2022). CRPL in gifted education that focuses on SMARTIE goals steers desired learning outcomes and appropriated skill development for beginner and advanced gifted educators. Culturally responsive leaders also use goal setting as a tool to evaluate continuous improvement for

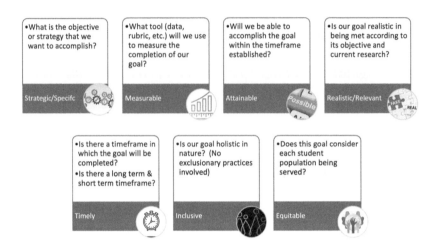

FIGURE 3.3 SMARTIE goals.

professional learning and growth. The feedback gathered from SMARTIE goal can provide leaders with valuable information to develop a CRPL experiences that are high quality and effective, considering each gifted student from a cultural capital, or strength-based perspective.

Professional Learning Communities

Honoring intersectionality and connectedness for meaning-making, we would be remiss if we did not include the topic of professional learning communities (PLCs) in the discussion of best-practices for CRPL in gifted and advanced programs. PLCs are defined as learning communities committed prioritizing planned collaboration and critical interrogation of learning practices in an ongoing, reflective, and growth-promoting way (Mitchell & Sackney, 2000; DuFour, 2010). For gifted and advanced educators striving to become more inclusive and equitable in their teaching practices for student learning, PLCs hold immense promise for modeling learning and for addressing consequential victimization and marginalization of student groups as a result of identified disparities and inequities. Learning together shifts the common practice of teachers working in isolation, creating a collective responsibility to adopt transformative (incorporating multiple perspectives) gifted teaching and learning practices that honor each student's learners' profile (academic readiness, interest, and cultural value). Effective communication, critically reflection and focus on student success, is key to an effective professional learning community in gifted and advanced learning (Roberson, 2024). The premise is in the title...its a community

As an experienced high school campus administrators and district-level coordinators we've always stressed the importance of establishing professional learning communities within gifted and advanced programs, giving educators space and time together to collaborate, cultivate new ideas, and to be vulnerable. We have found that informal peer mentoring relationships that naturally develop from dedicated time together with an intentional focus, has positive impact on teaching practices and retention, especially those new to teaching. To us, PLCs are a sacred space where organizational trust is built and strengthened; they ensure that all educational stakeholders have space and room to grow.

TABLE 3.1 Characteristics of an Equitable Professional Learning Community in Gifted & Advanced Learning

Strength-Based	Gifted and advanced educators move away from deficit thinking and towards establishing equitable teaching and learning.
Honest Discourse	Gifted and advanced educators are reflective in current practices and themselves to support student success.
Ongoing & Continuously Improving	Gifted and advanced educators have the commitment with action to match. Always looking to grow and improve the PLC process.
Strategic in Nature	Gifted and advanced educators incorporate data, SMARTIE Goals and topics to guide decision making.
Collaborative	Develop concrete action steps to implement inclusive practices in the classroom and school environment collectively as a unit.
Timely	Time is structured, dedicated and leveraged throughout the school year for gifted and advanced educators to actively collaborate.

Adapted with permission.

What Are the Non-negotiables?

Leaders in gifted and advanced programs in schools and programs serve as a catalyst to shift change and enhance the development and training of for educators through an optimal professional learning experience. As you consider the CRPL model, whether it on a K–12 campus, within a university teacher preparation program, or gifted organization events, the lens and foundation for your knowledge base and leadership development is critical and should be carefully interrogated. When creating a systematic process for professional learning, culturally responsive gifted leaders must provide a learning format that includes a) a foundational, well established, and shared philosophy for culturally responsive professional learning; b) culturally responsive resources, content, and materials for CRPL; c) access to diverse methods of training throughout the year that appropriately addresses the district's and campus SMARTIE goals; and

FIGURE 3.4 Recommendations for foundational professional learning needs as culturally responsive gifted leaders. Reprinted with permission.

d) formative and summative evaluation and feedback of professional learning offered annually.

These recommendations can serve as non-negotiables for creating a professional learning process in your school or district. A well established philosophy for culturally responsive professional learning is important because it communicates the "why" and fosters buy-in from stakeholders who must first understand the the priority and value for continuous learning and skill-development.' Integrating appropriate culturally responsive resources, content and materials, you want your gifted stakeholders' continuous learning to be supported by access to multiple opportunities and ways of learning and strengthening their professional craft throughout the year. Situations with family, personal circumstance, and personnel changes occur that require educators to also shift the priority and time commitment for their own professional learning. This is why it is important to have a a comprehensive system where professional learning is accessible at all times for anyone who desires or need it. This includes considerations for various modalities and platforms in which professional learning is received by stakeholders. In addition to standing PLCs and on-site workshops, offer individualized experienced- and grade-level synchronous and asynchronous learning opportunities to support personal schedules and preferred learning style. Making sure all content, materials, and trainers, are vetted as equitable, culturally responsive, research-based and up to date. This is vital to your program's success as a whole.

Lastly, ensure that the educators incorporate and maintain demonstrated growth and progress through their own a critical self-reflective lens. Find creative ways to capture their feedback and evaluate your professional learning processes. Doing this task ensures sustainability, longevity and informs program implementation policy for your program, sets the tone for all practices; policy must also be constantly evaluated for equity and inclusiveness. Inclusion is not an automatic consequence of a presence of diversity. Within any organization, there are two cultures of practice at play—that which is formally adopted or documented and that which occurs organically as a result of the systemic influence of individual beliefs and practice. Culturally responsive gifted leaders with an equity focus understands the importance of creating and modeling a culture of documentation with any new practice and steering away from undocumented practices. This awareness is critical when seeking to create a more inclusive and representative gifted program that equitably matches the district's student body. Diversity speaks to representation, but inclusion speaks to one's active and authentic engagement and evolves accordingly.

CRGL Leadershift

Ensure critical self-reflections by participants of CRPL as shared for personal to give contextual, authentic feedback for sessions and presenters. This will help you, as the culturally responsive gifted leader, to continuously improve your program in dynamic, timely, and most reliable ways.

Program Alignment

As a reminder, we put forward that equitable practices lead to equalized opportunities. Similar to the level of district-wide administration and oversight for special education and other 'title' protected programs, the development and/or restructuring of a gifted and advanced education program that is culturally responsive and equitable for equalized opportunities across all campuses within a district requires alignment. Alignment is a critical component when attempting to solicit and ensure systemic change. Programming should be aligned with and reflect the expectations that are outlined in a) state and district GT policy, b) district-level leadership vision for GT programming, c) school-based services and resources, d) financial support of CRPL and PLCs that are strategically connected to gifted programming, e) curriculum design and instructional practice and f) communicated or family/community co-designed models for whole-child development.

CRGL Leadershift

Utilize interest inventories and surveys to disseminate to gifted teachers and leaders and determine professional learning needs.

Work with campus leaders and district-level units on establishing vertical and lateral Professional Learning Communities. Collaborate as often as you can.

The first three of these alignment components are expressed at a broader leadership level—district personnel, chiefs, directors, principals, assistant principals of instruction/curriculum, etc. Developing and casting district-level vision is an important step that is as much about ensuring school level buy in that is necessary to ensure adequate infrastructure as it is in affirming and fostering shared understanding across schools and learning levels for gifted programming. Using the district's gifted program philosophy and vision as a foundation, campus administrators should be able to identify and align all of their building-level gifted services and resources, paying particular attention to those that they find to be the school's strength and/or those that uniquely position them to serve as a model for other schools in the district. These include, but are not limited to, core curricular, co-curricular, extra-curricular and community-based activities and partnering programming. Similar to equity audits, a simple landscape analysis using cultural capital (Bourdieu, 1977 as cited in Prasad, 2005) and funds of knowledge (Amaro-Jiménez & Semingson, 2011; Moll et al., 1992) as theoretical frameworks are a great way to evaluate a school's strength toward the gifted and talented development of its students.

Positive outcomes from district- and campus-level goals and expectations are met through the consideration within four major areas a) DEI&A-focused research (Diversity, Equity, Inclusion, and Access), b) Inclusive policy, c) Documented and undocumented beliefs, values and practices and d) two-waycommunications. It is important to note that DEI&A-focused research supports researched-based practices as well as a four-tiered level for evaluating those practices (see Chapter 5). We recommend whenever possible, that district leaders sanction a CRPL research team designated to ensuring accountability (also referred to as task force) for promising practices in the scholarship of teaching and learning (SoTL) in gifted education. A CRPL task force should include an advanced level gifted professional or faculty member who leads participatory or action-based research for the district. A CRPL task force can design, conduct and even publish findings of small-scale, pilot and/or case-study research. Participatory and action-based approaches are the most appropriate. Participatory approaches include those that are closest to and/or active contributors in curriculum development and implementation. Action-based approaches, as a component of SoTL, include formal and/or informal professional development training, including training the trainer models and professional learning communities (PLC). While not meant to be all-inclusive, sources and/or models for practice include participatory, action-based, small-scale, pilot and case-study research.

CRGL Leadershift

Build up teacher leadership by developing teacher leaders in your schools and district to present to their peers on gifted and advanced education topics. You want gifted subject matter experts (SMEs) to talk and build up other future gifted experts.

Leverage the differences in the community each school serves. Collaborate with other district-level units and campus-level departments (SPED, multilingual education, counseling, etc.) for conducting training sessions, share resource and expertise, and broadening understanding of the intersectionality of gifted RCELD students.

Social and Emotional Implications

Professional learning is the cornerstone by which lifelong learning for educators exists and is essential for anyone positioned as a teacher, coach, or mentor. The extent to which they are equipped to be culturally responsive has consequences beyond students' academic preparation and performance. Underrepresented students in gifted education that do persist in gifted, advanced and STEM education often find themselves feeling isolated, underserved, stereotyped, lacking reflective mentors and struggling to successfully navigate in spaces and institutions that are well represented with White students and dominant culture value systems. Therefore, just as important are these social and emotional contexts of learning (Collins, 2015; Ford et al., 2018, 2022) that impact whole-child development and self-concept in gifted education.

Conclusion

Concerning the human development of the whole individual, culturally responsive professional learning (CRPL) promotes consideration and integration of the social, emotional and cultural (SEC) contexts of talent development for underrepresented individuals in gifted education (Collins, 2015). CRPL not only equips gifted and advanced education professionals with the foundations needed for robust teaching, but also builds students skills to promote individual resilience vital to persistence in gifted, advanced, STEM and higher education as a whole.

Questions to Critically Self-reflect on During Your Journey

1. As a CRGL and teacher leader, how do you understand and help other teachers recognize their own cultural biases?
2. For the sake of inclusion, how will you incorporate student meaning-making and authentic learning tasks into CRPL? gifted programming? classroom curriculum?

3. How do you encourage a standardized practice for integrating multiple perspectives (transformational approach) into the curriculum, instruction and student engagement? CRPL? Policy for gifted programming?
4. What does giving students a 'voice' look like within your leadership role in gifted and advanced education?
5. How do you honor the reported experiences of inequality of students and teachers even if you do not fully understand them?

4

Beyond the Status Quo

Fostering Culturally Responsive Curricular
and Instructional Experiences for
Gifted and Advanced Programs

Education as a means to freedom requires more than changes to the
curriculum. True transformation takes place when there are changes to
pedagogy.

-Dr. Bell Hooks, 1994

When thinking about instruction and curriculum which are
inclusive in gifted and advanced education, culturally respon-
siv gifted leaders must believe that it goes beyond content. Each
student needs to feel like they matter. Students need to feel seen
and be at the heart of the advanced level classroom. Their lived
experiences and their academic achievement should be at the
forefront of everything educators do. For too long, RCELD students have not been exposed to curriculum nor instructional support that utilizes their communities, stories and truths. Students
have been subjected to only a single Euro-centric perspective
of society: American and world history within the US education system. This has created oppressive structures for students
of color when learning through curriculum and the teaching
practices of educators. The absence and underrepresentation of
histories, truths and contributions of various BIPOC individuals
and communities in their education, specifically advanced level

DOI: 10.4324/9781003374923-4

learning, has left a gap in honoring true academic fidelity. For years, we, as Black leaders in gifted and advanced education, have heard educators state 'Oh, we celebrate Hispanic/Latinx Heritage Month" or 'I always include Dr. Martin Luther King, Jr., Rosa Parks and Black authored books in my February lessons for Black History Month.' Simply adding these activities and assuming inclusivity is occurring pushes the agenda of equity being mandated versus embedded in the culture of the gifted or advanced program. Our gifted students deserve better. Our gifted students deserve more. When there is a curriculum where our students are not seen or heard, the curriculum has failed to be inclusive of each child. This is why the leadership behaviors and decisions of gifted leaders are important as they can either foster an environment of change towards equity or replicate oppressive structures and continue its perpetuity throughout the program. Leaders in gifted must not only raise questions and concerns about the curricula being used in their programs, but ensure that they themselves are equipped with the tools to shift the 'status quo' for systemic change. Implementing and developing high quality and equitable gifted curriculum and instructional support for teachers involves transformation in mindset going beyond our educational past, beyond politics and beyond what we always do- to better reach and serve each gifted learner.

Culturally Responsive Pedagogy

In the 1990s, culturally responsive pedagogy was developed as a means to address underachievement in students from diverse backgrounds as a means to strengthen student learning outcomes. Drs. Geneva Gay and Gloria Ladson Billings (1995, 2010) were integral scholars in creating a framework for culturally relevant pedagogy and culturally responsive teaching, which many researchers in the field believe are the foundations to culturally responsive pedagogy (CRP). Culturally responsive pedagogy is multidimensional, validating and comprehensible. It not only encompasses instructional practices but also student-teacher relationships. Learning context, assessments, curriculum, classroom management and overall classroom climate (Gay, 2010). Culturally responsive pedagogy is meant to empower students and enrich their everyday lives in and outside the classroom.

Gay (2010) expanded on culturally responsive pedagogy and shares that educators who were culturally responsive utilized six dimensions:

♦ Culturally responsive teachers are socially and academically empowering by setting high expectations for students with a commitment to every student's success.
♦ Culturally responsive teachers are multidimensional because they engage cultural knowledge, experiences, contributions and perspectives.
♦ Culturally responsive teachers validate every student's culture, bridging gaps between school and home through diversified instructional strategies and multicultural curricula.
♦ Culturally responsive teachers are socially, emotionally and politically comprehensive as they seek to educate the whole child.
♦ Culturally responsive teachers are transformative of schools and societies by using students' existing strengths to drive instruction, assessment and curriculum design. Culturally responsive teachers are emancipatory and liberating from oppressive educational practices and ideologies as they lift 'the veil of presumed absolute authority from conceptions of scholarly truth typically taught in schools.' (Gay, 2010, p. 38)

When educators incorporate cultural responsiveness into their classroom, they are promoting equity and serving as change agents in their school and district communities. These individuals are catalysts for positive reflection of diverse students in curriculum and instruction. Culturally responsive education uses prior experiences, knowledge and culture references to validate and empower student success through academic and extracurricular subjects. We know this shift in mindset is needed throughout education, especially gifted education as so many students simply are not connected to the education they are receiving. Culturally responsive educators in gifted education can provide a sustainable learning experience for each type of gifted student, especially those who are RCELD.

CRGL Leadershift

Be sure to include anti-racist and culturally sustaining teaching pedagogy within curriculum and instruction.

Involve all key stakeholders (parents, district and campus leaders and students) in your biannual and annual program evaluation processes.

What Culturally Responsive Pedagogy in Gifted and Advanced Learning Is Not

Now we've talked about the benefits of being a culturally responsive gifted educator. What we haven't focused on is what it isn't. We believe this is a great time to note that although many believe they are being culturally responsive in their practice, in hindsight they are incorporating something totally different. Addressing a few (not all) of the misconceptions and preconceived notions that we've encountered is something we believe is important for anyone striving to be more equitable as a culturally responsive gifted leader.

A big misconception is that cultural responsiveness is all about race. With the current political climate on all things diversity, equity, inclusion and belonging in education, many have automatically assumed anything equity driven, like cultural responsiveness, focuses solely on race. Yes, race does encompass a portion of CRP, but not all. Culturally responsive pedagogy is multidimensional. It harnesses the experiences, cultural assets and knowledge of students from diverse populations. Those backgrounds include race/ethnicity, language, religion and economic status to name a few. Another misconception is that the educator must be an expert in the student's culture. This too, is false. Educators must build a relationship with students to know and learn about their culture but not be experts in it. Going beyond the surface of cultural variants of students by building a deeper connection is what can help educators grow in cultural responsiveness.

Being culturally responsive also does not require you to have the same background as your students. You can be Black, White, LGBTQ or even have religious diversity and still be culturally responsive and equitable. This journey involves a paradigm shift in the stakeholder's mindset. You are making a commitment to combat injustices of all kinds and to understand how RCELD students have been historically and systematically oppressed over time. This will allow you as a leader to interconnect with these understandings and develop an appreciation for them. Your role is to support varying populations in advanced level programs and help ensure all students within those populations can achieve academic success.

Lastly, cultural responsiveness in giftedness is not only for diverse students. Although very beneficial for those students of RCELD backgrounds, cultural responsiveness is a best practice to incorporate for all students. Culturally responsive education fosters a learning environment that is student centered, rigorous and builds critical thinking skills. These few attributes can provide meaningful and engaging learning opportunities for advanced level students.

So...Where Do I Start?

As a gifted and advanced leader striving to be more equitable in curricular and instructional decisions for your program, you are probably thinking about how to start this journey. We believe that this journey first starts with a critical self-reflection of current practices in curriculum and instruction. Being honest with yourself, your teachers and students about what's presently being implemented in the program and how. Leaders must come to terms with their own underlying assumptions and the possible prejudices they may have and that may occur within

TABLE 4.1 Sample Questions to Consider When Critically Self-reflecting on Gifted/ Advanced Curriculum and Instruction That Needs to Be Equitable

Critical Self-reflective Questions for Gifted Leaders on Curriuclum and Instuction	
Does the current curriculum and instructional prograams used in our program prescribed or authentic?	Are our teachers creating a classroom environment that is nurturing and inclusive to each student?
Am I honoring the families and cultures (and future/potential) of the students within the program through teaching and curricular practices?	Does the rigor of the courses reflect student interest, ability and stamina?
Am I considering the classroom layout (flexible grouping, cooperative learning, etc.) of the learning environment?	Do our teachers still implement modeling, scaffolding or any modifications for a challenging curriculum? (Also for a varied type of learner)
Do our teachers build on student strengths and use them as a starting point for learning?	

their program knowingly and unknowingly. Honesty is the best policy in this case. That way, gifted and advanced leaders can become more critically conscious of their program, policies and curricular and instructional decisions.

Critical self-reflection in gifted and advanced leadership requires a shift in how the individual leads, their behaviors and overall thought processes. The reflection can include reviewing materials, teaching frameworks, conducting equity audits and building awareness for other stakeholders involved. This in return creates a pathway for meaningful conversations that grow our gifted educators and ourselves in the process. Although critical self-reflection alone will not be a quick fix to inequity within advanced level programs, it is a start. Many leaders embarking on being culturally responsive in gifted and advanced learning may feel this work is challenging. This work can be challenging for some and a breeze for others. But it is doable and possible for those who want to do the work. In any situation, being critically self-reflective in an advanced level program urges leaders to grow for future learning opportunities. As an education leader, you learn something new everyday. You are learning how to transform your program for the better. As previously mentioned, it takes a paradigm shift and being willing to become a change agent to transform your advanced level program where equity is at the forefront of all you do.

What Would You Do?

Ebonee had a vision. As a veteran gifted educator and leader, she knew how important it is for gifted students to learn from educators who adapted, modified and planned accordingly to support the gifts and talents of students. She also recognized the value of students connecting to curriculum and instruction with their lived experiences. The 6th–8th grade state standards received an update for math and science subjects. Ebonee created a plan to update the gifted curriculum that aligns to the standards. She knew that developing a comprehensive curriculum that aligned to state standards would not only receive more buy-in from leadership but also needed to be challenging and in-depth to connect to students. It also needed to measure student growth and progress and include a plethora of instructional strategies that cultivates high achievement and talent development in gifted students. She knew she could not update the math and science gifted curriculum alone so she reached out to all gifted math And science teacher leaders in the district and set up meeting times and plans to collaborate on this much needed update. She knew she needed the support of campus principals and district leaders so she reached out to them sharing the following: a proposal of the gifted curriculum updates for math and science, a timeline of events, the purpose and goal of the updates, the individuals needed during the process and possible cost of substitutes, materials, etc. Her district serves 12 middle school campuses. Eight of the campuses agreed to send teachers to help design curriculum while four were still on the fence and questioned the value or importance of the update in general.

1. *What do you believe Ebonee should do as a next step to connect with the four principals on their apprehension?*

2. *Do you think Ebonee should reach out to the district math and science leadership for support? Why or why not?*
3. *How often do you align and update curriculum and instructional practices in your district? Are they inclusive?*

A Holistic Approach

Equitable curriculur and instructional support for gifted and advanced programs must have an inclusive and holistic approach at the core of its implementation. This belief is steered towards serving the varying types of gifted learners. We look at this work with an 'each versus all' standpoint. Gifted scholar Ken Dickson speaks of this notion often in his prese. With any work in education, terms like 'each' and 'all' are important. We want all gifted students to get access to quality education. We believe all gifted students have the ability to do great things through our programs. The term 'each', however, denotes a more specific approach to students who are served in gifted. The each versus all debate actually conceptualizes the 'equity versus equality' concept. As we know, when dealing with equity, it is fairness that is more specifically based on individual difference or need. Equality is fairness for all. In gifted, yes, we want to serve all students. But the concept of all focuses on the larger group at hand. Equity focuses on each student and what each student needs in order to be successful. That is the holistic approach culturally responsive gifted leaders must take when supporting their teachers and curriculum used. Inclusivity through each and not just all.

Within the gifted curriculum and instruction, we know there are some non-negotiables that must be addressed for student academic success. The 2019 NAGC Pre-K to Grade 12 Gifted Programming Standards (2019) list some concepts that are incorporated in quality gifted curriculum and instruction. These concepts include a) being learner centered, b) depth and complexity, c) develops students' talent, d) use evidence-based instructional strategies in delivering curriculum, e) is rigorous and challenging,

f) responds to the diversity of this world and g) is adaptable. These structures also align with state and national standards and can measure student growth and learning outcomes.

While we agree that these are extremely important aspects of gifted and advanced curriculum and instruction and should be integrated as such, culturally responsive gifted leaders should build on this foundation to include all the previously mentioned attributes and add the following:

♦ Reflects, respects, acknowledges and values various cultures and the prior experiences of gifted students extending the learning experience where needed; intentional and meaningful representation of diversity of this world within materials.
♦ Is accessible for each gifted student regardless of environment.
♦ Models high expectations but has the support to match the expectations.
♦ Recognizes systemic biases and inequity and puts measures in place to mitigate them, not contributing to the status quo.
♦ Evolves to the child it teaches to.
♦ Is real world applicable to the environments, communities and neighborhoods of 21st century gifted students.
♦ Is collaborative and flexible in nature with families and communities being served.
♦ Is adaptable and modifiable with consideration to specific student needs and populations (2e, 3e, MTSS, Multilingual learner/emergent bilingual, Culture, socioeconomic status, race/ethnicity, etc.).

Gifted education leaders seeking to become more equitable can utilize culturally responsive gifted strategies in the classroom to create an optimal learning environment that is sustainable for their program and for each gifted student.

4 Rs of Culturally Responsive Education in Gifted Classrooms

Throughout this chapter, we've discussed key concepts that are essential to optimal teaching and learning in a culturally responsive gifted classroom. A major component of a high quality, equitable gifted curriculum also includes how content is taught through pedagogy. Gifted teachers must be able to connect the curriculum to the lives and lived experiences of gifted students, especially those from traditionally underserved backgrounds. A great teaching strategy to consider when striving for a more equitable approach to gifted teaching is the 4 Rs framework (Davis, Floyd & Roberson, 2020). The Four Rs (relationships, representation, rigor, and relevancy) guide educators' efforts in creating an instructional environment that is culturally responsive for gifted students from traditionally underserved student groups.

A positive relationship an educator has with a student can make or break any connection that student has with school itself or school programs. The trust built with that bond is powerful. Many times, the educator is the only person a student may have in their life that cares, encourages or even supports them. This is why when lesson planning and creating a culturally responsive learning environment in gifted, you must establish positive, respectful relationships with students. These relationships can serve as catalysts for forging future connections with students'

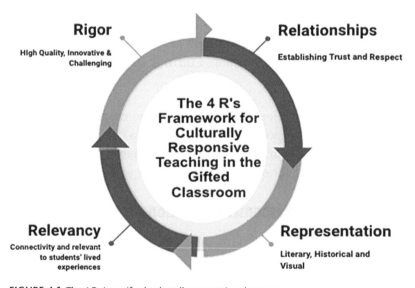

FIGURE 4.1 The 4 Rs in a gifted culturally responsive classroom.

families, communities and more. It may sound cliché but the truth is simply talking and listening to students is a great start to understanding the population you are serving. This interaction could lead to collaborative efforts on class projects, input on classroom literature and more. An increased positive relationship could also build representation in your gifted program. RCELD students are historically underrepresented in gifted and advanced level programs. But developing positive rapport with RCELD gifted students and their families could create a pipeline to increase nominations and referrals of possible GT students to the program.

As students and teachers build relationships in the culturally responsive gifted and advanced level classroom, they also want to visualize themselves in the curriculum and content being taught. Representation is ensuring that all students, regardless of diversity and background, are represented in the learning environment. Students want to see themselves in what is being taught. From the pictures to the modeling and as well as texts, having those classroom materials present can make students feel valued, respected and seen.

While collaborating with students, to promptly improve your relationship and their representation in your gifted or advanced program, rigor must also be included as a means to provide challenging, yet meaningful tasks to any lesson to increase critical thinking skills and go beyond basic levels of understanding. As many believe the word rigor means 'more work' or 'harder difficult tasks,' it's actually the opposite. For the culturally responsive gifted and advanced level classroom, rigor involves more in-depth and complex aspects of lessons so students can have authentic challenges that push their thinking outside the 'box.' This type of work engages students to explore new learning, new ways to think and to problem solve. It incorporates higher order thinking skills, authentic assessments and real world inquiry-based learning. Adding rigor also includes differentiation academically, through social-emotional learning and modifications according to what your high ability learners need to be successful.

Lastly, gifted and advanced teaching that is culturally responsive needs to be relevant. Gifted and high potential students from

RCELD backgrounds want, need and thrive in a learning experience that aligns and values their lived experiences. This type of teaching does not focus on a singular euro-centric view of education. It provides students the opportunity to be shown that they matter—their communities, their voices, their experiences matter enough to be incorporated in lessons learned by the entire class. This is critical in culturally responsive gifted teaching. Because traditionally underserved students are underrepresented in gifted, they need relevant tasks, assignments and assessments connected to the world we live in—which includes their communities, their language and their culture. This way, students will know their learning experience has purpose and reason. Relevancy is also an equitable practice as it builds on prior knowledge of students, helping students connect emotionally to what they already know with new content being introduced. We need gifted and advanced level students students to feel and believe that their learning is directly connected to them and their lives.

CRGL Leadershift

Connect frequently with your school's or district's literacy department for texts, books and primary and secondary resources to support embedding culturally responsive resources for students.

Utilize educational technology, online tools and apps to create engaging lessons and activities that connect with real world experiences for gifted students.

Conclusion

Infusing gifted and advanced-level teaching and learning with equity at its core takes dedicated leaders, educators and stakeholders. Students learn best when they are connected to the curriculum, their lives, their struggle and their community. They also learn best when taught according to their needs and adaptable as they are at the center of the learning experience. Although disproportionate in representation for decades, for RCELD students, the intentionality of culturally responsive gifted and advanced curriculum shows recognition and understanding that these students too, do matter, are valued and are seen. Gifted and advanced level leaders play a crucial role in sorting, implementing and developing a holistic approach to equitable instruction and curriculum for these dynamic groups of students.

Questions to Critically Self-reflect on Your Journey

While thinking about how our gifted and advanced teachers and leaders can utilize the curriculum, instructionand pedagogy in a way that is equitable for each student, here are some questions to consider when making decisions:

1. As a culturally responsive gifted leader, how will you be intentional in integrating student perspectives, histories and communities in your gifted curriculum and instructional practices?
2. What resources can you use for supporting a highly viable and equitable gifted or advanced level curriculum in your program?
3. What culturally responsive practices do you currently see in your gifted or advanced curriculum and instruction?
4. Since you are on the equity train with other stakeholders in your school, district or university community, how will you empower those individuals with adjustments needed to the gifted curriculum and instruction?

5

Representation Matters

Using Data To Guide Decision Making

Engaging in critical dialogue and culturally responsive pedagogy allows data based decision making to be framed within an equity context.
-Park et al., 2013

The gaps, injustices and other controversial issues surrounding gifted education policy and practices have been a topic of research and discussion since the inception of gifted education and continue to be more so today. In addition to the lack of progress within the social orders of our American society at large, there is also the issue of scientific racism that has played a major role in justifying racial inequality supported by the authority of science as objective knowledge and acultural processes. However, as briefly introduced in Chapter three, the 'acultural myth'—the belief that something or someone lacks culture and/or cultural influence—has led to erroneous beliefs in an existence of acultural policies and practices that become partially normalized and erroneously standardized as well. That myth is also, unfortunately, perpetuated by a colorblind ideology which further marginalizes minoritized communities (Collins, 2018, 2021a).

An equitable gifted and advanced level leadership approach is needed to steer away from a colorblind ideology as it is detrimental to our field. Evans (2007) discusses how colorblind ideology

DOI: 10.4324/9781003374923-5

and approaches to leadership can provide the rationale for institutions of learning to ignore issues of diversity and the benefits that may come from exploring them. Educators that promote a color-blind approach refuse to identify equitable and equalizing outcomes for students of color. These individuals refute the concept of recognizing and understanding differences in how learners and educators have experienced schooling in society. Educators who profess color blindness lack the requisite racial knowledge to successfully teach students of color and struggle to account for the full identity of their students in the process (Gooden et al., 2015; Collins, 2018). Color blindness in education can perpetuate a status quo that a white euro-centric perspective is the only valid educational perspective. In return, this conserves a cycle of inequity that minimizes the experiences of people of color even through instructional and curriculum support in schools.

Centering gifted and advanced educator discourse around race, cultural influence and disparities amongst student groups can benefit the learning experience as this brings awareness and attention to factors educators may not have had initially. Understanding how these factors affect gifted and advanced programming, policy and ultimately data can shift leadership viewpoints from deficit-centered gaps to strength-based growth and improvement. There needs to be a system where accountability, data analysis and culturally responsive practices are at the forefront for continuous improvement in schools and special programs (Roberson, 2023). Cultural responsive gifted leadership has the capability to impact policy, procedures, systems and structures that refute inequity and create pathways to inclusivity and socially just practices.

Mining the Data: The Gifted Referral and Nomination to Service Delivery Process

Researchers who study phenomena within marginalized groups are likely to make false assertions and interpretations when relying solely on prior theoretical frameworks that often ignores typical development within non-mainstream groups. In addition, the selection and use of intelligence (IQ) and academic achievement tests in the identification process of racially, culturally, ethnically and linguistically different students for special education programs are fraught with controversy, limit consequential validity and diminish fairness in the assessment process (Collins, 2021a; Graves & Mitchell, 2011). Consequential validity refers to credibility in terms of accuracy and validity that the ideas and meanings intended by the research are consistent with interpretations and practices translated (Collins & Roberson, 2020). Understanding the consequential validity issues of research that are translated into practice is critical. Research has continued to evolve with increased diversity of student populations, and the validity of test measures and their development in gifted programming continue to evolve as well. Therefore, the need to design referral, identification, service delivery processes and overall policy that are culturally appropriate measures of giftedness and talent is also critical for program growth and equitable student group representation. Salient cultural variables should be included in this creation of measures as well as updated local policy and decision making to guide implementation.

But Where Do We Start?

One of the most important decisions an advanced level leader committed to equity makes is ensuring their practice reflects policy, and vice versa. Leaders must look at the ways in which the nomination and referral process begins for possible identification of gifted students. If we want to cast a wide net in identifying untapped potential from all student populations, leaders need to have policies and procedures that ensure their identification processes do just that—reach each type of gifted learner. Yes, we know there is no perfect policy nor procedure within gifted and advanced level learning. There are, however, solutions that are equitable and are capabie of yielding significant positive outcomes for identification of students from diverse backgrounds.

The ideal policy that is developed is free from deficit ideology and stereotypical 'status quo' referents. It supports stakeholders

FIGURE 5.1 Big ideas for policy development in gifted and advanced learning for culturally Responsive Gifted Leaders.

in seeking talent using cultural capital and student background as assets (see Chapter 3). The policy creates practice that seeks talent utilizing, integrating, and/or considering the student's home language and cultural values. This ideal policy ensures talent can be recognized from students in all economic statuses without victimizing those from low-income statuses (Collins, 2022a). It recognizes talent regardless of circumstance and is systemic in nature while being equitable in its practice. In other words, this type of policy has three big ideas, or constructs, built in its purpose—access, opportunity and equity. We believe if gifted leaders maintain consideration for these major factors at the forefront of policy development, programs can positively flourish. Culturally responsive gifted leaders (CRGLs) aiming to become more equitable in their leadership understand the critical impact that nomination procedures and logistics have in identification of potential gifted learners; they ensure that the application process is a) easily accessible all stakeholders and the public in general, recognizing that those that come in constant contact with potential students include parents/guardians, extended family member, community leaders, mentors, and/or other stakeholders; b) implemented with several opportunities and multiple modalities so that the nomination procedure is shared in a timely manner along with important information and reminders associated with it (i.e., important deadlines, etc.); and c) equitable in terms of seeking evidence of talent to include broad and inclusive artifacts, two-way communications in primary home languages, and so on.

TABLE 5.1 Guidance for Gifted and Talented Nomination and Referral Documentation Policy Development

Nomination/referral application must be available and accepted in numerous languages (seek translators - in case online translations are sometimes may be inaccurate)	Nomination/referral must be open to all stakeholders as teachers, parent/Guardians, extended family, community members, counselors, staff member, students' peers, the potential student, etc.
Nomination/referral application must be easily accessible via online and/or print. at the schools and major community institutions.	*Nomination/referral window is best open at least between 30-60 days (2 months) or longer, if needed, and considerate of local holidays recognized*
Community and family meetings on nomination/ referral and identification benefits and process are offered in person and virtually. throughout the year.	*Professional learning opportunities on nomination and referral are available to educators in person and virtually.; training should include discussions around contextual, typical and atypical manifestations of giftedness*
Nomination/Referral application should include important demographic data for responsive identification source selection. (e.g., birthdate, student district and state ID, grade, schools attended, primary language at home, parent/guardian name and contact information, nominating individual's name and signature, observation prompts using standardized measure, space for qualitative narratives and characteristic checklists)	Allow nominators to submit and accept self-selected evidence with explanation to support any listed criteria and/or quantitative measures.
	Whenever possible, include universal screening measures
	Utilize campus and district data to support nomination/referral of potential gifted students and share with campus leadership
	Storage location of completed applications need to have virtual and physical copies for documentation purposes (some states require you keep documentation for an extended time)

CRGLs also acknowledge that it is best practices to identify and support these same notions to establish policy criteria for equitable gifted nomination, referral and identification.

In alignment with these factors, CRGLs also existing school and/or academic data to support new referrals may or may not have missed opportunities for identification. As such, administrators should explicitly calculate and share equitable indices indicative of expected representation from diverse student groups. They take into account the current student body and be sure all stakeholders have access to information about the various ways characteristics of gifted learners may be manifested from all representative backgrounds in age and cultural background. Doing both of these will also help decision-makers to identify any disparities beyond statistical error. One of the many factors in underrepresentation of RCELD students in gifted and advanced level programs is nominee limited or restricted knowledge of the traits and behaviors of giftedness. This limited foundational knowledge is due, in part, to lack of professional learning, awareness and even implicit bias about what constitutes evidence of giftedness by certain groups of individuals.

Implicit bias refers to the attitudes or stereotypes that affect our understanding, actions and decisions in an unconscious manner (Ford et al., 2016). Stakeholders can develop assumptions of certain student groups, their academic abilities and behaviors and connect them to students' intellectual identities involuntarily, and erroneously. This can lead to stereotyping student groups unconsciously, resulting in negatively affected adult behaviors, understanding and expectations of students. While implicit bias may be unintentional or may not align with an individual's beliefs in educating gifted students, it can have detrimental effects on the nomination, referral and assessment of RCELD students in advanced level programs. In a study of referrals of Black students for gifted services, Grissom and Redding (2016) found that even when Black students have the same grades and test scores as their White peers, educators are often suspicious of them and underestimate their abilities, resulting in under-referrals for gifted education nomination and screening. Leaders in gifted and advanced level programs need to help educators understand, identify and address implicit bias as it can serve as a barrier for student access to gifted and advanced programs; as mentioned in Chapter 3, PLCs are a great way to do this. Training and awareness for gifted educators and stakeholders on gifted characteristics of students from marginalized and minoritized groups can eradicate this inequity and support strategies to assist in increasing student referral numbers. Cultivating an inclusive classroom environment and being critically self-reflective in identifying any discrepancies in their process or current practices to nominate students are just a few topics leaders can embed in culturally responsive professional learning (CRPL) support throughout the year to aid in addressing bias in gifted and advanced education.

Universal screening is also an option in addition to and/or in lieu of referral or nominations. This process includes administration of at least one formal identification measure (e.g., ITBS) to all students in an identified grade level as the first step of identification assessment (Lakin, 2016). Universal screening has many advantages including students having the opportunity to be identified even if they were not nominated by a stakeholder. This option, however, can become costly and should not be used to exclude students from the nomination process. If the financial resources allocated to your school or program allow for universal screening, that option has the capability of increasing chances of students from RCELD backgrounds being identified for gifted and talented services, and to find more students in general.

CRGL Leadershift

Seek training to become familiar with a wide variety of ways giftedness is manifested. Expand and open your trainings beyond gifted teachers and leaders; on-level classroom teachers and administrators will also benefit.

Assessments in K–12 Gifted Programming

Many types of assessments have been known to be used to identify children as gifted and talented. However, single testing and more comprehensive assessments have a long standing history in bias and discrimination towards marginalized student groups in education and gifted education (Ford, 2016; Roberson, 2020). As previously mentioned, traditional test measures such as intelligence (IQ) tests have been known to be used as a sole assessment measure to identify giftedness; However, IQ tests are known to be racially biased, and a single test does not equate to a complete assessment. Achievement, ability/aptitude and intelligence (IQ) tests are all noted to be used as criteria to measure giftedness in schools and programs across the nation. Multiple assessment criteria that align to varying gifted characteristics of students will best serve a gifted and advanced program. Quantitative and qualitative measures can support reliability and validity within a student's gifted assessment data. It is imperative that the assessment measures used to identify gifted students from various populations are inclusive in nature, culturally unbiased, and that a wide array of tools are used so they can holistically offer a the gifted profile for a student.

Is there an ideal assessment that can be used specifically to identify gifted RCELD students? We are asked this question a lot as Black gifted scholars in the field. Many educators want to know if there is a quick fix or a single test that is 'most equitable.' Although there are a multitude of assessments currently that leaders can choose for their gifted program, we believe that question (and its response) is multifaceted. Equity is a journey that can take time even with comprehensive assessments. If a company make claims that the test they publish is 'the most equitable' on the market and guaranteed to close the opportunity gap in underrepresentation completely in gifted, you should follow-up with additional clarifying questions and ask for that guarantee in writing; if they can provide neither, think twice about investing in it. Equity requires systemic effort and change. There are multiple factors that should impact assessment selection, and that affect equitable outcomes for identification and retention of RCLED students in gifted programs. Finding, creating or implementing an assessment that you believe best fit your student body is a first step and great start because assessment(s) are only as good as meeting the identification needs for who is being served? Do the assessment(s) measure academic achievement and creativity? Do they possess qualitative and quantitative attributes? Do they account for students who are linguistically and economically different? Is the assessment(s) reliable, valid, and consistent? What is the RI (representative index) for the students identified - to what extent do the students identified match the overall student population of the school? The district? These are just a few important factors to consider when seeking the answer for what is the ideal assessment(s) for your program.

When thinking of how CRGL committed to equity should approach and choose assessments for gifted students, we also believe they should consult and embed the guidance from the most current research on gifted students of color specifically (e.g., see Grantham et al., 2020; Ford et al., 2021, 2022; Cotton et al.,2022). Representing the decades of collective research and experiences of its authors, The Culturally Responsive Equity Based Bill of Rights for gifted students of color (2018) addresses advocacy, access, program evaluation, testing, curriculum, social and emotional development and family and community empowerment (Ford et al., 2018). The focus of these concepts was directly used to address prevalent issues gifted students of color face. It serves as a framework for how educators use these concepts in building culturally responsive and sustainable assessment practices for gifted programs. All eight sections are focused and recommended for gifted educators to use as a viable tool for support.

We felt it important to share with those on the path of cultural responsiveness in gifted and advanced programs as one of our many resources. For evaluation and assessments, these Black scholars in gifted education believe each RCELD gifted and potentially gifted students have:

◆ *The right to a culturally, racially and linguistically diverse/different gifted education assessment committee.*
◆ *The right to general education, special education, preservice and current professionals trained and dedicated to recognizing and valuing their expressions of gifts and talents.*
◆ *The right to be evaluated and identified using multiple criteria.*

- *The right to be evaluated in multimodal and multidimensional ways.*
- *The right to be assessed with non-biased tests and instruments for screening and identification.*
- *The right to be assessed with nonverbal tests for screening and identification.*
- *The right to be evaluated by bilingual test examiners (e.g., school psychologists).*
- *The right to be assessed by tests and instruments in their predominant or preferred language.*
- *The right to be assessed by tests and instruments translated into their primary or preferred language.*
- *The right to be assessed with culturally normed checklists.*
- *The right to be evaluated with tools re-normed to represent their cultural experiences and realities.*
- *The right to be evaluated by tests and instruments normed on students of color for screening and identification.*
- *The right to be assessed by tests and instructions normed locally.*
- *The right to educators who adhere to official testing and assessment policies and procedures.*

(Ford et al., 2018)

We assert there is no one 'perfect' assessment for the RCELD gifted student. What we do know is that CRGL must have a paradigm shift in how they approach assessments and the practices aligned to and informed by them. Several multi-faceted considerations are critical when deciding which assessment criteria best aligns with the student body as well as the with the purpose and specific assessments, and the offerings and services within the gifted program itself. Assessing to identify a student as "gifted" is different from assessing to identify students for services designed for gifted and and talented programs. This distinction is important in how you present finding for assessment as well as your decision letter to the student and their family. Think about it from a services and student perspective: What services do your offer? Does the assessment serve as as indicator for giftedness and/or inclusion into the programs you offer? Does your program utilize "cutoff" scores? Are the purpose of the cutoff scores to qualify a characteristic of giftedness, and are these scores appropriate to the services you offer. If you only have an after -school co-curricular program for gifted students, certain assessments and/or a strict top 5% percentile ranking require-ment may not be appropriate as criteria to accept that student for services. Consider also a scenario where, you have a child who is new to a school and is referred or nominated for gifted services. When is the most appropriate time and most appropriate assess-ment based the child's educational background up to this point? How will the child interact with the assessment(s) in this new environment? Are the assessments inclusive in nature based on the child being assessed? Was the parent/guardian and student provided information about the program and given an opportu-nity to prepare for any testing included in the complete assess-ment? Have you ensured assessment(s) available in the student's primary language spoken in the home? Are the conditions that you give the assessments conducive to their learning/evaluation environment?

CRGL Leadershift

When using local or building norms, steer away from achievement assessments as a data measure if they are biased in nature or disadvantages RCLED students.

Identification and Placement

Nomination, referral and single testing are only prerequisites and the initial step in the assessment process. An formal evalu-ation of the data gathered for the nominated student must still take place to formally identify a student as gifted an/or place-ment for appropriate services. Once all nomination and referral information is gathered and collected, and other assessments have been properly administered, the next steps and process move to the identification and placement phase of gifted and tal-ented students. Service and program design options for gifted and advanced programs differ from state to state. They also vary among schools in districts and within a city or state. Keep in mind all of the service and programming considerations for nomination and referral are important and can inform identification and placement. Be sure you have a gifted and talented placement committee with members who are formally trained and locally oriented in data dissaggregation to identify and place students. If you are in a large school system, it's best practice to have a placement committee designated at each campus. These individuals may interact with students each day and are familiar with who they are in general. If you are a district level leader, you need people that are 'boots on the ground' with the program and the students being assessed. As a centralized or district-level leader, you most likely can only go by the statistical data given to you. These stakeholders can attest to students potential even more if their day-to-day interactions involve supporting them. Here's a general guide for the makeup of a gifted placement committee:

♦ Campus-level gifted teacher (1–3).
♦ Campus administrator (i.e., principal, assistant principal of instruction, instructional coach, Gifted Coordinator etc.; 1–2).
♦ Central office gifted coordinator or Curriculum & Instructor director (1–2).
♦ Counselor (1–2).
♦ Community member (if possible; 1–2).

As the culturally responsive gifted leader, it is your duty to make sure the committee is collectively made of individuals who are properly trained in areas including, but not limited to: gifted education pedagogy, identifying and serving RCELD students in gifted, social/emotional and cultural needs contexts of gifted and talent development, nature and needs of the gifted, gifted and talented assessments to include nomination/referral, and gifted service design processes. Having these foundational tools within your placement committee builds and maintain a strong, equitable assessment, identification and placement process.

CRGL Leadershift

Local norming also serve as a responsive and equitable framework or standard for identification in your school or district.

Many school systems use rubrics and checklists during gifted placement meetings. With any meeting regarding decisions for students, as an equitable gifted leader, always set the purpose for the meeting. There is power in setting purpose, as it articulates awareness. Discuss the goals of the program, why it is vital to have everyone at the table for this decision and what opportunities can be provided for a child if identified. This is such an important responsibility for everyone involved as a child's learning path will be affected. Make sure everyone feels welcomed, respected, valued and ensure the environment is positive! You should be excited to come together on behalf of students! Yes, this is serious but it's also a labor of love and work of the heart. You all are not just there to determine if students are placed to receive gifted services, you are impacting the trajectory of how they will foster their potential in years to come. Be proud that you are to this point and celebrate! Good vibes only, leaders!

Now that the tone and purpose of the placement meeting is set, it's time to dig into the details. A rule of practice we've experienced success with during placement meetings is sharing a SWOT analysis of the gifted program and having a SWOT analysis of each student that qualifies for gifted placement. A SWOT analysis is usually used in corporate companies as a tool to analyze what they do best, devising a strategy for the future depending on both internal and external factors (Mind Tools, 2023). SWOT usually stands for strengths, weaknesses, opportunities, and threats. However, we've switched up the typical meaning of two of the letters to come from a strengths-based approach aligned with giftedness and equity.

When determining gifted placement using the gifted SWOT analysis, the committee will address and discuss student strength, which is the 'S.' This is not just in academic and tested areas but also in other areas like fine arts, leadership and creativity. We know giftedness comes in different forms and can be expressed in ways within and outside of core academic areas. The committee must use this information when making placement decisions. For the 'W' we've replaced the word weakness with 'ways to support growth.' We believe every child has untapped potential and also areas that they need more support in. Committees can analyze and discuss this information during meetings as well. The 'O' stands for 'opportunities to thrive.' Using the strengths and other data shared, the committee will collaborate on how the student can thrive from in-depth and complex gifted experiences from being identified. This could include creating an individualized gifted education plan and giving strategy super from a strengths-based approach. If a student has a set of skills, the committee can gather resources for talent development of those skills and more. Lastly, instead of the word 'threats' for the letter 'T,' we choose 'thoughtful awareness.' We have to be mindful of our students' lived experiences, home life, languages, gender,

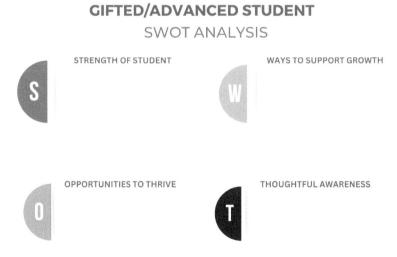

GIFTED/ADVANCED STUDENT
SWOT ANALYSIS

STRENGTH OF STUDENT   WAYS TO SUPPORT GROWTH

S   W

OPPORTUNITIES TO THRIVE   THOUGHTFUL AWARENESS

O   T

FIGURE 5.2 Gifted SWOT analysis for placement meetings.

learning disabilities (if any) and the intersectionality of these factors when determining giftedness. Developing a positive gifted learning experience that is foundational in these aspects is a recipe for success!

Along with the aforementioned factors, incorporating local norms is an equitable measure for gifted leaders. The issue with national norms is that many times they do not attest to the students in the district or even the school building. Using local norms for your student groups denotes more specificity and equity. Local norms can cast a wider net for identifying students. As you use norms to determine placement, utilizing an equity formula like the 20% or 80% rule can serve as a positive attribute in supporting equity in your program (Collins & Kendrick-Dunn, 2022). Ford (2013) stated equitable representation in gifted education could occur if a race/ethnicity group's proportional representation in the gifted education program is at least 80% of the group's total representation in the student population of the school or school system (Wright et al., 2017). This also could apply for a special population if needed based on the total representation in the school of program. So where does the 20% come from? The designated 20% accounts for factors such as human error, data measurements and assessment policies that have the capability of being potentially biased. Another method still using the 20% rule is calculating 80% times the total number of a specific population in the district. That sum can also give you a suggested proportional representation for that specific population in gifted.

What Would You Do?

Kayla is a brilliant, Black 3rd grade student at Shane Elementary School. She is creative, thinks outside the box, is inquisitive and completes her work within units of study with a score of 95 or above on a scale of 100. Amy, Kayla's 3rd grade teacher, thought she would be the perfect candidate for referral to the school's gifted program. In Amy's state, in order to nominate students, you must have parent permission to have students assessed for gifted and talented identification. Since she knew many parents were unaware of how the gifted program works, she decided to host a parent meeting and invited all parents and community members. She reached about specifically to Kayla's mother. Amy hosted the meeting and got a great turnout! However, Kayla's mom didn't attend. Amy knew she needed Kayla's mother in attendance to get approval for Kayla's nomination. She reached out to her individually and spoke with her after school one day as she was picking up Kayla. Amy began explaining about the program details and nomination needs. 'Kayla is a creative and high potential student who I think would definitely benefit from gifted services,' she shared. 'I really believe she would greatly benefit from gifted services here at our school. She's been nominated for gifted testing. We need your approval to assess her as we think this is a great opportunity for Kayla. Can we get parent approval from you, please?' Kayla's mother looked in worry. 'I don't think we should test Kayla for gifted right now. She's already an "A" student and I don't want her to have more work to do. Plus, I wasn't in gifted when I was in school…why does she need to be in it?'

1. *How should Amy respond to this parent in a way that is not only considerate of her point of view but also the parent's position?*
2. *Would it benefit Kayla's mother if Amy hosted another parent meeting or forum specifically for her? Why or why not?*
3. *What resources can Amy provide Kayla's mother to support her reasoning for her nomination to the gifted program?*

Advanced Academics

For secondary gifted and advanced students matriculating through middle and high school, their path also encompasses various options of rigorous and relevant coursework. Many states refer to these course options as Advanced Academics or Advanced level programs. Advanced Academics includes courses, programs, assessments, services and supports that provide opportunities for students to demonstrate college, career and military readiness and earn postsecondary credit. Program and course options including the following (but are not limited to): Advanced, Honors and Advanced Placement (AP) courses, International Baccalaureate (IB) and Dual Enrollment. Advancement Placement (AP) and Dual Enrollment (DE) are the two most popular programs that allow students to earn college credits while in high school (College Board, 2017). These course and program options provide access and opportunity to all students. However, they too, have experienced underrepresentation and disparities amongst minoritized students. In 2015–2016, Black students represented approximately 15.4% of U.S. public school enrollment, but only 9.4% of those enrolled in at least one AP course (U.S. Department of Education, Office for Civil Rights, n.d.). Similarly, Xi et al. (2021) found in the 2015-16 and 2017-18 dual enrollment participation rates by the Civil Rights Data Collection (CRDC) that White students participated in dual enrollment at almost twice the rate of Black and Hispanic students (Xu et al., 2021). Advanced Academics have served as a pipeline for gifted students to take advanced coursework on the Secondary level. However, because we have witnessed inequity towards minoritized students at the elementary gifted level, this is also a contributing factor to their lack of participation and enrollment in many of these course options.

It is because of these systemic disparities that Culturally Responsive Gifted Leadership can also be applied to supporting Advanced Academics. Although many of the courses serve students not identified for gifted services, we still believe these supports are a viable resource for leaders of these programs as well. Although course requirements vary from state to state, a secondary high potential and gifted student can greatly benefit from these programs. Remember, CRGL is a framework for any leader serving an advanced level program. If you serve in the secondary leadership capacity, you will be familiar with the aforementioned course options. The gifted SWOT analysis, equity audits, stakeholder committees and policy creation can also apply to Advanced Academics. Equitable practices are needed in these areas as the data shows underrepresentation, access and opportunity has been an issue for decades.

Evaluating Advanced Programs Using a Culturally Responsive Framework

In a system of standardized curricula, educators must be careful not to bolster a classroom environment that is 'diversity-unfriendly.' For example, Shiel (2017) declared that designing and using performance tasks enhances student learning and assessment by promoting the critical thinking that students need in a standards-based educational environment. However, we posit that performance tasks that encompass problem-based or 'real life' exercises that are far from reality for culturally different students are not effective at all, and not enticing enough to pique the attention and/or desire for enrollment of RCLED students. Without some deliberate teacher or intervention, what is presented as a culturally neutral environment will continue to play a major role in exempting advanced programming from BIPOC students' self-selected option for further development. Collins (2022) contended that performance tasks must:

1. Be free of verbal bias in the form of unnecessary or unexplained difficult language and/or culturally unknown terms.
2. Be free of stereotypes that can otherwise be inflammatory and/or emotionally charged.
3. Illustrate fairness in materials, portrayals and representation of CLED students in a range of roles.

Underrepresented and historically marginalized students who have encounters with STEM (categorically considered as advanced academics) content, resources and opportunities can feel disconnected and disadvantaged if information presented is culturally and racially void or contains little to no consideration for their cultural capital, values and interests. We know that a student's STEM identity is positively or negatively impacted by the extent to which his or her perspective is centered around and culturally connected to the content in which they are learning (Johnson, 2012; Varelas et al., 2013). Even more, cognitive diversity suggests that differences in perspective, as a by-product of cultural differences, cultivates creative problem solving and innovation that should be appreciated and valued as a resource for contribution (Basnight-Brown et al., 2023; Gerkin, 2022; Qi et al., 2022). In her report to NASA NGS (Next Generation STEM) leadership, Collins alluded that NGS and its educational products were in a unique and global position to guide authentic STEM experiences that critically shape and positively influence students' STEM identity, motivation and persistence in ways that can build a significantly more diverse NGS workforce. NGS recognized the importance of deliberately seeking opportunities to increase cultural relevance that fosters diverse ways of knowing, understanding and presenting information to ensure diversity, equity and inclusion (Collins, 2022b; Collins et al., 2022). As such, NGS and NASA EPDC under Collins' leadership set a collaborative goal to align all existing products with national DEI&A (diversity, equity, inclusion and access) initiatives, to include diverse populations' perspectives to existing content, and to ensure opportunities for culturally valued meaning to the NASA content. Content was evaluated using the culturally responsive framework that Collins had utilized in her graduate level courses. Their goal was to build capacity for curriculum developers to self-assess their own work for cultural responsiveness.

Collins' Four Culturally Responsive Levels

Collins (2021a) distinguished between culturally relevant (Ladson-Billings, 1995), cultural responsiveness (Gay, 2000) and cultural sustainability (Paris, 2012), noting that pedagogies in multicultural education have changed their stance, terminology and practice over the years. As the term suggests, culturally relevant includes relevant material and/or information that is relayed with culture as a vehicle for sharing, teaching and learning. Culturally responsive indicates the importance of evaluation and responding to it in a culturally appropriate manner. Culturally responsive, then, is a way of communicating and messaging that recognizes the importance of including a cultural context (e.g., knowledge, experience, performance styles, etc.) in all aspects of information gathering and dissemination for the purpose of making information encounters more relevant and effective for RCELD students. In addition, it also takes into account harm and harm reduction—no student should be disadvantaged by content that is insensitive or disrespectful to their cultural identity; educators must take great care not to victimize their students—encouraging a perspective that portrays the marginalized student as the source for their marginalization. Collins proposed that culturally responsive evaluation (CRE) is an extension of culturally responsive teaching (Ladson-Billings, 1995).

Generally speaking, we've utilized the principles of diversity, equity, inclusion and justice (DEIJ, or JEDI as it is sometimes referred) as a checklist to evaluate the culturally responsiveness or NGS content (see JEDI definitions and other key terms for shared understanding at the end of this chapter). When developing, implementing and evaluating information, documents and/ or performance tasks, curriculum developers and instructors must ask the following:

a. Diversity: Is the content representative of target populations and diverse identities? Is it multiculturally situated?
b. Inclusive: Does the content promote authentic, strengths-based participation and build participants' multiple perspective competencies?
c. Equitable: Does the content allow participants to successfully complete tasks even if expressing an atypical viewpoint or process?
d. Socially just: Is the content absent of cultural minimization, dehumanization, victimization and culturally problematic presence within the social construct?

Based on the answers to these questions and the extent to which information, material, performance task and so on are presented bias-free, stereotype-free and with fair representation—creating a seven point nominal checklist, we've purported that all content can be classified at one of four culturally responsive levels, with level one being the lowest and most detrimental:

1. Culturally destructive: Reinforces stereotypes and/or portrays people of color as inferior and destructive.
2. Culturally insufficient: Contains little to no consideration for cultural diversity; culturally and racially ambiguous.
3. Culturally emerging: Represent information in some diverse ways.
4. Culturally responsive: Represent information in widely diverse and culturally dynamic ways.

If curriculum designers, assistant principals of instruction and/or other evaluating officers find that the material or task does not meet the satisfactory culturally responsive level that has been pre-determined by their authority, then a more comprehensive evaluation can be conducted to find the more specific issues. (See Collins' 37-point checklist and CRE Comprehensive Evaluation Tool included at the end of this chapter; Collins, 2021b).

Conducting an Equity Audit in Gifted and Advanced Programs

Another evaluation tool we recommend is an equity audit. Equity audits examine trends in data, analyze current policies and assess culturally responsive pedagogy, curriculum and overall practices in education (Khalifa, 2018). Auditing processes are a pretty typical educational evaluation method. But putting equity at the forefront of an audit does not happen as often as we'd hope. We believe an equity audit of curriculum and instruction, policy and even professional learning of gifted and advanced teachers serves as a continuous improvement growth measure.

Equity audits can bring awareness and support decision making for school and program leaders on instructional and curricular practices, policy and data holistically (Roberson, 2023). Since the majority of gifted programs are served within school systems, leaders can apply this tool when evaluating their program as a benefit to the school and district community as they are transparent, informative and essential to progress. Equity audits can be beneficial to gifted programs as the disparities within

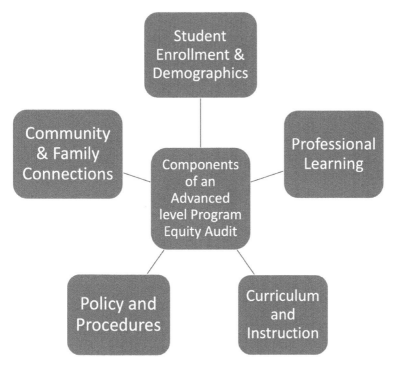

FIGURE 5.3 Sample key areas for an equity audit in advanced level programming. Reprinted with permission.

traditionally marginalized student groups and their representations have been continuous for years. Culturally responsive gifted leaders can utilize equity audits as a means to build their gifted program to reflect the population of the students being served holistically and as a growth measure for future program planning.

As a result of equity audits, gifted and advanced leaders will have the ability to use the data to develop SMARTIE goals. I'm sure you've heard of SMART goal setting as a general in education practice. The acronym SMART stands for specific, measurable, attainable, realistic/relevant and timely. The letters 'I' and 'E' are added to include inclusivity and equity. SMARTIE goals can support equitable outcomes desired for students and create timelines that are aligned to gifted and advanced level program needs (Roberson, 2023). These goals are meaningful, specific and build you and your program's commitment to equity. This can

Student Enrollment and Demographics	Professional Learning	Curriculum and Instruction	Policy & Procedures	Family & Community connections
Total Enrollment by Campus/District Total enrollment by Student demographics (Race/Ethnicity; English Learner, SPED/504, Low SES, etc. 5 year data of program enrollemnt	Current options for teachers and leaders Alignment with State and national standards Data on amount of professional learning and areas received by stakeholders	Curriculum writitng processes Materials, frameworks, etc. currently used (Teaching and instruction) Curricular/Instructional standards alignment with State/National standards Review of processes to support various student populations in curriculum/instruction (accomodations for SPED/504, English Learners, etc.)	Assessment, Identification, Nomination and Referral procedures Data for Assessmeent, Identification, Nomination and Referral outcomes Mission, Vision and current goals of program Professional Learning requirements Entrance/Exit Policy Recruitment & Retention efforts	Parental advisory committee Community Events & partnerships Included in Policy for Family/Community Involvement Resource support for Gifted parents

Reprinted with permission.

serve as a catalyst for change with you as the change agent spearheading this important cause. Instead of equity being tolerated in your gifted program, it is in the fabric of its DNA.

CRGL Leadershift

If a principal is struggling to conduct gifted testing on their campus, bring the testing to them and conduct it for them!.

Evaluation meetings once you conduct an audit should be a time of reflection, honesty and goal setting based on all types of data accumulated. If you see a pattern or trend, mention it. This is not the time to be timid or embarrassed because of what is found. Supporting program growth is key!!

Questions to Critically Reflect on During Your Equitable Decision Making Journey

Utilizing data to support policy, assessments and practice in your gifted program is a vital need as an equitable gifted leader. You set the tone of your program through policy, the documents supporting policy and procedures to follow. When creating these avenues, ask yourself the following questions:

1. Are your current policies for gifted identification inclusive in nature to consider each student?
2. When do you believe an equity audit can best serve your advanced level program?
3. When using the 37-point checklist on assessment, curriculum or any entity you chose, how will you disseminate the findings to stakeholders?
4. How will the SWOT analysis aid stakeholders in viewing students from deficit-free thinking?

6

It Takes a Village

Culturally Responsive Gifted Leadership and the Power of Partnerships

Trusting partnerships among families, communities, and schools are critical to accomplishing "the complex task of educating a diverse group of students in a changing world"

-M. Tschannen-Moran

One of the most powerful factors in developing a successful gifted and advanced program is the inclusion of partnerships. Family, community, school and stakeholder partnerships have the capability of bringing sustainability to the program. As a leader moving through the realm of equity, it's vital that these individuals be a part of the journey. Culturally responsive leaders cannot improve the educational experiences of RCELD students without positive stakeholder relationships (Roberson, 2020). You have to establish partnerships for the growth of your gifted and advanced program. These individuals, just like you, want what's best for each child—socially, emotionally and academically. As we focus on the value each stakeholder group brings in this chapter, we also want to share strategies to support their input within your program. Essentially, partnering and collaborating with various stakeholders through equitable efforts helps us help students reach their goals.

DOI: 10.4324/9781003374923-6

The Value of Parent and Family Engagement

Family and community members play an important role in talent development and improving academic outcomes for gifted and high potential RCELD students. The relationship schools and districts have with families also has the potential to positively impact student achievement and students' social and emotional well being. Parents may not see how important they are to this process in the beginning of the child's academic career in advanced learning. Some parents may think they don't play a big part in their child's educational experience outside of the classroom. But as a culturally responsive gifted leader, you know that narrative is false. You believe in the power of collaborating with families and the progression that will bring for the students. It's your job to help foster positive relationships amongst families in general. We have been fortunate to work with parents of students ranging from kindergarten through 12th grade and post secondary. We believe that leaders need a strategy to keep family engagement a priority in their gifted and advanced programs. When focused on equity within family involvement, the 6Cs can aid leaders in this process.

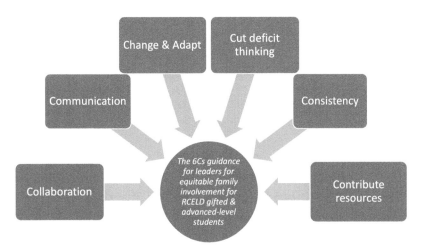

FIGURE 6.1 The 6Cs in equitable family involvement for RCELD gifted students as guidance for leaders.

Communication

In any relationship, being able to communicate effectively is always a high need in education. For gifted and advanced RCELD students, parents and families keep leaders and stakeholders informed on student needs beyond the classroom into their communities and home life when we are being communicated with. Having an awareness of student needs can determine if the need could have an effect on the students' success in th program. Ensuring we are active in our communication efforts to them about our program and resources builds positive interactions and associations with school and home. Equitable gifted and advanced leaders use multiple means of communication as you consider who is being served in your program and school community. Offering on campus and virtual options for parent meetings, including translators for families and translating text in more than one language exudes inclusivity. Also, remember to use verbiage that is inclusive when communicating to families. For example, in newsletters, instead of saying 'Dear Parents,' state 'Dear Parents, Guardians and Families' when addressing the school community. You must value those individuals, their circumstances and their cultural tenets. Leaders welcome various points of view when communicating goals, policy and procedures in gifted. Engaging in meaningful dialogue and discourse supports program growth.

CRL Scenario

Zach is a guardian of Analeese, an 8th grade student recently identified in the gifted program. He is struggling to see the benefits of gifted and advanced academics as his child transitions from middle to high school. He is a single father of two who is very active in his childs education but wants to learn more about the benefits of the program. The gifted campus coordinator, Trey, reached out to Zach after talking with him at the latest parent forum for newly identified students in the district. 'I think this is a good program but do they even have GT classes at the high school?' In their district, gifted students are served at the elementary and middle school levels with specific, sheltered gifted courses. Once they transition to high school, gifted students can enroll in honors, AP and dual enrollment courses and receive enrichment through those courses according to the state plan. He has had parents complain to him about the 'lack of a gifted experience' secondary gifted students have faced in the past.

1. *How should Trey respond to this question?*
2. *What resources can Trey provide the guardian so they can feel more comfortable about the high school gifted experience for Analesse?*
3. *If there is a shift that is needed in the district or campus, what can Trey do to get buy-in to make the shift to support gifted secondary students?*

Collaborating for the Greater Good

Collaborating with gifted and advanced level families is also an effective strategy that promotes inclusivity. As a culturally responsive gifted leader, you must utilize parents and families as your educational partners. They are the gateway to insight into your student's home life. Families are able to reinforce anything that is being taught or established at school. Leaders can provide families with tools that can help students at home. This in return, could increase student motivation and engagement in class. A few tools that parents/guardians can collaborate with their school to support gifted and advanced level students include:

◆ Reading to and with students a variety of texts.
◆ Volunteering at school or in a classroom.
◆ Supporting goal setting for gifted student achievement.
◆ Collaboration through decision making (voting in school elections).

- ◆ Have meaningful conversations about school and talking about their day.
- ◆ Check on assignments and homework regularly.
- ◆ Communicate high realistic expectations for gifted children but ensure the support is there to match the expectation.

Equitable gifted and advanced level leaders also collaborate with families on current and upcoming events, any community needs and even legislation pertaining to gifted students. Many times, it's families and the school community that identify, advocate and nurture the talent of their children. The benefits of family collaboration with gifted and advanced programs and schools are limitless.

Consistency Is Key

Consistency within the program is indispensable and a high need. Families need consistency as a way to show that culturally responsive gifted leaders only change according to the program's needs and they respect the time and effort the families provide. Attending parent meetings and events, responding to communication sent and volunteering in various ways all take the parent relying on their child's school program to be consistent, only changing when deemed necessary. Being consistent through equitable practices in a gifted program requires gifted leaders exhibiting a number of behaviors, including insisting that the gifted environment is welcoming throughout the program. Think about how you are able to retain RCELD students and their families. They need to feel like they belong in your program. For years in gifted and advanced learning, underrepresentation has placed a negative view of RCELD representation in these programs. It's your job as the leader to ensure these students and their families know that they are wanted, needed and valued. Being consistent in the program's mission and vision as well as its communication and collaborative efforts shows that change is welcomed and needed.

CRGL Leadershift

Connect with local businesses about internship opportunities for gifted students. These opportunities are especially beneficial to students from vulnerable and/or underrepresented populations (i.e., low socioeconomic status, Multilingual learners, 2e/3e students, etc.).

Build the parent/family partnership through consistent communication to include student progress and school/classroom events. At the beginning of the school year, introduce yourself and make it be known that you desire to build a positive relationship for the success of their gifted child.

Cut Deficit Thinking

As a leader seeking to become more equitable in gifted and advanced learning, we encourage you to use critical self-reflection of yourself and your program as a growth measure frequently. Through this reflection, leaders are able to identify, reflect and respond to any deficit views one may have of certain student groups, families, cultures and circumstances. This includes helping others identify these deficit views they may hold knowingly or unknowingly. Some scholars believe that having deficit thinking or views of students involves blaming students or their families for their lack of success or them being a burden to educators because they are deficient (Shields, 2013; Valencia, 2010). Deficit views of students also include having negative perceptions of students, particularly those of color or from low socioeconomic backgrounds, and them being inferior to the dominant culture. These views are meant to demean traditionally marginalized students. It looks to blame students and their families for achievement gaps rather than focusing on the positive cultural assets and tenets they bring. Deficit thinking looks at languages outside of English as barriers versus assets to education. It can build on stereotypes of people living in poverty but not mention the systemic inequities that placed students or their families in that socioeconomic background in the first place. Culturally responsive gifted leaders have to disrupt this mindset. If educators or other leaders (including yourself) form biases and assumptions about families, you must recognize it and work to mitigate it as it is a barrier to equity within a gifted program.

CRGL Leadershift

Connect with the school's or district's counseling department for social and emotional support of gifted students at school and home.

Train and encourage parents/families to look for and combat perfectionism traits in their gifted child. Encourage risk-taking, metacognition and learning from making mistakes as strategies for growth; this can lessen the need for perfection with which many gifted students struggle.

Change and Adapt When Necessary

Each year and possibly every quarter, plan on working with stakeholders for checkpoints of the program. You could form a parent/family gifted council or advanced academics association with stakeholders in the community and schools. This is an opportunity for youto positively connect with families and stakeholders of your gifted and advanced program. They can provide input, recommendations and overall support to make your program better. You want every voice heard and valued. If changes are needed, you can hear straight from the stakeholders who are impacted outside of the classroom. Remember, the goal is to improve and grow your program for longevity, to recruit and retain students for a successful learning experience. These individuals can help this process. If anything needs to change, it's a part of program growth to make it better.

Contribute Resources

With any community and family partnership, you must provide resources to support families at home with their gifted child. Parenting a gifted child is already a task that sometimes can be overwhelming in itself. Without any support, the everyday frustrations and fears of parenting can create feelings of resentment or loneliness in the gifted parenting journey. It may be difficult for gifted parents to connect with other parents within a school community or with gifted leaders in general. Gifted parents need to be educated on giftedness, advocacy and resources available to them. Culturally responsive gifted leaders adhere to this need. Families need guidance on how to reinforce what gifted students are learning at school and at home. Assisting families with navigating the school's website, keeping up with social media updates and getting them on the school's mailing list are just a few ways to contribute as a resource. Offer resources in multiple formats so they may be accessible to parents (i.e. synchronous and asynchronous). Parents and guardians also need to be informed about their rights pertaining to their child's education. Some gifted students may receive special services including 504, special education and dual language support. Culturally responsive gifted leaders can share this information along with any other important legislation related to their child's gifted services. Leaders also share community resources for students' at home success, such as educational-based family needs organizations, referral programs and community health organizations for family needs. Parents and guardians are the child's first teacher before anyone else. It's vital to make sure they have access to resources for home life to strengthen the home-school connection.

The Importance of Community Partnerships

With any education partnership, the school community at large plays a major role in its relationship. Families, schools and the larger community are strong, interconnected influences on students (Lockhart & Mun, 2020). Culturally responsive gifted leaders understand the value the community brings to schools and special programs. Those connections can set students up for college, career and community leadership for the future. Gifted leaders could create a community resource handbook that is regularly updated and easily accessible for parents and families. The book could include up to date information on community resources such as housing, social service organizations, health organizations and even legal assistance to name a few. Leaders can also invite these community organizations to parent nights and events that are hosted throughout the year. We believe that having positive relationships with community members and encouraging educators to make meaningful connections with them will positively impact kids in the long haul.

CRGL Leadershift

Encourage parents/families to look for and maximize their gifted child's strengths while addressing areas of improvement; broaden the accepted sources of strengths beyond core academic areas.

Consider the family dynamics (cultural values, background, membership, etc.) of all gifted students, and responsively communicate and offer resources accordingly.

Reimagining University Educator Preparation Programs

We've discussed many elements related to being a culturally responsive gifted leader and sustaining an equitable gifted and advanced program through family and community partnerships. Another vital stakeholder to gifted program sustainability is university partnerships. University teacher and leader programs prepare future educators of the gifted for entry into the greater world of education. By collaborating, university preparation programs remain current regarding school and program practices pertaining to advanced academics and gifted programs. The universities also receive an opportunity to view and experience program culture and climate. Field visits to parent meetings, professional learning and campus events ensure that university personnel get a first hand view of 21st century gifted and advanced level programs. University and educator preparation programs can benefit from this type of collaboration to better prepare inexperienced leaders in implementing cultural responsiveness in the learning environment. Leaders must ensure that universities are up on the most recent best practices, current issues and legislation related to gifted students and their impact on schools and programs.

Conclusion

As we look to focus on the matriculation of gifted students from primary through secondary and on to post-secondary, the family and community relationship holds the key to success. Families are vital in the process of identifying and developing students' exceptional abilities, as well as providing emotional support to maximize talent development throughout their academic careers (Olszewski- Kubilius et al., 2018). As a culturally responsive gifted leader, you must set priorities and goals for this partnership along with the other concepts expressed in this book to accomplish. It may not always be the most wanted decision but the outcome can change the trajectory of a child's life for the better.

Remember, becoming a change agent requires a paradigm shift. Research tells us that implementing culturally responsive leadership behaviors in gifted and advanced level programs can influence the academic achievement of RCELD students (Roberson, 2020; Khalifa, 2018; Roberson & Floyd, 2020). If gifted and advanced leaders want to address systemic inequities and disproportionality that have saturated the field of advanced learning for years, it is critical that they themselves become culturally responsive in the process.

Questions for Critical Self-reflection on Your Journey

As you think about the behaviors of culturally responsive gifted leaders and ways to connect with the families and the community at large, consider the following questions to ask yourself:

1. How do you develop meaningful and positive relationships with your gifted or advanced level families? The community in general?
2. How can you ensure your gifted and advanced level teachers create an environment that is welcoming to all families and stakeholders?
3. When families don't see the value in gifted programs, what will you do to support the child's future in the program?
4. Create a family and community plan of action for your program with your gifted teachers by using the form in the index. How can this goal be a tool for collaboration with families in your program?

Afterword

A Call to Action: Implementing Culturally Responsive Professional Learning: The Leader as Change Agent

Susan K. Johnsen, PhD

While the United States grows more diverse, minoritized students continue to be underrepresented in programs for gifted and advanced students. As Roberson and Collins mention in their introductory chapter, less than 4% of Black students and less than 5% of Hispanic students are identified as gifted as compared to nearly 9% of White, and almost 13% of Asian students (Gentry et al., 2022). Moreover, only 2% of Black students and 8% of Hispanic students are enrolled in advanced level math courses (Coffey & Tyner, 2023).

To empower campus and school district leaders in building a more diverse student population within gifted and advanced programs, the authors have provided important information about culturally responsive gifted leadership practices. They focus their attention on the characteristics of students from diverse backgrounds, the use of culturally appropriate measures, methods for referring and retaining RCELD students in gifted and advanced programs, designing a culturally responsive curriculum that incorporates students' lived experiences and involving the family and community.

What might encourage the implementation of these important practices? Banwo et al. (2022) mention four specific leadership behaviors that drive cultural responsiveness within a school: critical self-awareness, culturally responsive curricula and teacher development, culturally responsive and inclusive school environments and engaging students and parents in community contexts. All educators need to be aware of a) the differences between school-centric and community-centric expressions of

DOI: 10.4324/9781003374923-7

education, b) knowledge derived from personal experiences, c) how environments affirm or negate identity and d) ways the community can provide culturally appropriate knowledge. How do leaders develop these areas of cultural awareness and responsiveness? How do leaders teach educators to be critically self-reflective? To use culturally responsive curriculum? To promote inclusive environments? To engage authentically with the community?

The process of change is complex and personal. Change generally begins with pressure from inside or outside the system—an awareness of a need—in this case, implementing culturally responsive practices—and then a decision to do something about it. According to Rogers (2003), after the decision is made to do something about the need, the individual must learn what it is and how to use the practices correctly before deciding whether to implement the practices.

To effect change, VanTassel-Baska and Johnsen (2017) described these important principles (see Johnsen et al., 2021 for further discussion):

> *Principle 1. Involve high quality people who are knowledgeable about the components of the change.*
> *Principle 2. Involve all levels, with each having distinct roles in the collaboration process.*
> *Principle 3. Clearly describe and model the required changes.*
> *Principle 4. Establish successful models in the early phases of the change process.*
> *Principle 5. Implement professional learning at all levels that encourage individuals' beliefs that they can actually implement the changes.*
> *Principle 6. Provide human and material resources.*
> *Principle 7. Improve practices at all levels.*
> *Principle 8. Provide continuous evaluation over time.*
> *Principle 9. Build trust with transparency*
> *Principle 10. Address and remove obstacles.*

Professional learning can integrate these principles and be an important stimulus for change. In my experience with implementing change, I discovered the following professional learning model was effective in creating the educators' awareness of a need and might also be effective in implementing more culturally responsive practices.

After graduating with a master's degree in special education and teaching in public schools for six years, I moved to one of the largest school districts in the country to develop and implement a program that would 'mainstream' special education students and integrate the schools. It was the early 1970s. Even though the Brown v. Board of Education of Topeka decision had occurred more than a dozen years earlier, the schools were still in the process of integrating children and faculties. When I arrived, more than 7,000 special education children were on the waiting list to be tested for services and the Education for All Handicapped Children Act (94-142, now IDEA), which required schools to serve children with disabilities, had not yet been approved by Congress. There were challenges.

What did our leadership team do first? We listened and found the administrators and teachers who would develop model schools and establish professional learning centers that exemplified differentiated practices responsive to each student's strengths and needs (see Principle 1). The three model schools were to be situated in different areas of the city for easy access and to indicate that the classroom practices were for *all* schools and *all* students (see Principle 2). During the first year, we established one of the Teacher Development Schools by collaborating with the principal and the teachers in implementing evidence-based practices in each of the classrooms (see Principle 3). Using our experiences, we developed and provided professional learning for all of the educators, involving administrators and support services. Support personnel who participated in the professional learning during the first year included psychologists, counselors, special education teachers and other educators who would provide direct and indirect services to children and those who would be involved in assisting educators in changing their practices (see Principle 7). Along with the teachers, we also developed practical material resources such as classroom assessments, self-paced curriculum, interdisciplinary units and independent and enrichment activities (see Principle 6). Depending upon the teachers' selected goals, they used these material resources to support changes in their instructional practices.

As we learned in collaborating with all of these educators, beliefs that emerged from lived experiences were important in adopting evidence-based practices (see Principle 5). Participants needed to be exposed to the effects of current practices and then be introduced to more differentiated methods. We therefore established a series of five progressive classroom systems that modeled essential characteristics of a differentiated classroom, with the first system providing non-examples (e.g., all participants doing the same learning activities) to the final system providing examples of a classroom that was differentiated for each participant (e.g., participants working individually and in small groups to learn at their own pace about content that was of interest to them). At the conclusion of each of the systems, the participants reflected and evaluated their experiences in terms of how they were grouped, the quality and types of learning activities, the teacher and student's use of time, use of assessments, teacher and learner decisions and participants' feelings about the entire experience. At the conclusion of the three day professional learning experience, participants were ready to set goals for changing practices in their own classrooms. They learned from these lived experiences that they needed and wanted to differentiate to provide services to children in their classrooms. They established goals based on their current level of differentiation and areas they might want to differentiate next (see Principle 8). We also involved the principals and the school's community members in the same professional learning experiences prior to the teachers so they understood the process and were able to support the teachers in selecting goals, providing resources and changing practices (see Principle 9).

Following the third year of implementation, evaluators from the RAND Corporation confirmed the effectiveness of the professional learning activities (e.g., the progressive classroom systems), collaborative goal setting, follow-up and institutional support on teachers changing their practices. This success led to the replication of this model in over 20 different states. Some replications included its use in Minnesota, with the implementation of the Southeast Alternatives Project in the Minneapolis ISD where students, parents and faculty were provided choices to develop experimental programs; with the Menominee Native Americans in Wisconsin in establishing a more culturally responsive education for their children; in Professional Development Schools, to develop collaborations between universities and school districts; and in a Javits grant focused on the implementation of differentiation in Texas rural communities (see Johnsen et al., 2002).

The curriculum, which was disseminated in a modular format during the professional learning, varied based on the campus or school district's goals. For example, in the large school district, we addressed classroom management, special education and differentiation whereas in the Javits grant, we focused primarily on identifying and serving gifted students in rural districts. We designed curricular modules related to learner differences and characteristics of gifted and advanced learners, organizing curriculum, assessment, managing the learning environment, instructional strategies, the teacher's role, mentoring, peer coaching, collaboration and technical support. Within the curriculum, participants had choices not only of the content (e.g., specific instructional strategies) but also how they might learn the content (e.g., independently, small group, reading, playing games and so on) and at what pace. Modeling these classroom practices and having participants actually experience the practice encouraged them to select their goals for implementation.

In the case of culturally responsive leadership and in building a more diverse student population within gifted and advanced programs, the modular content might address beliefs about different cultures and races, culturally responsive practices, building an equity-based culture, positive behavior support models, identifying gifted students from underrepresented groups, differentiating curriculum and instructional strategies, using formative and ongoing assessments, collaborations within and outside of school and developing community partnerships.

The progressive classroom systems that incorporate essential characteristics of culturally responsive teaching, both examples and non-examples, might move from activities that do not relate to the participants' lived experiences (e.g., using content of a different minority group than the ones participating in the professional learning activities) to group-paced learning activities (e.g., small groups do the same activities at the same pace) to activities that are more culturally responsive and relate to each participant's interests (e.g., use of assessments to identify strengths and needs; working independently or in small groups with participants who have common interests). The participants' critique of each management system might include the degree that it a) focused on their unique experiences and perspectives— bridged the gap between home and school life, b) was based on individual differences and equity, c) used positive behavior support rather than exclusionary models, d) matched their learning strengths and preferences, e) increased collaboration and f) developed relationships,

Culturally responsive gifted leadership requires culturally responsive professional learning. For leaders to institute change and increase the representation of RCELD students in gifted and advanced programs, they must develop learning opportunities where each participating educator personally experiences alternative models that increase their understanding of the important characteristics of an equity-based culture. Based on these experiences, educators will not only understand why they need to be more culturally responsive but will *want* to implement best practices.

Appendix

Sample Equity Audit for Curriculum and Instruction in Advanced and Gifted Classroom

Auditing Checklist and Questionnaire for Advanced Level Programs (Curriculum and Instruction)*

Please place a check under the corresponding box and provide evidence where suggested.

Element	Developmental & Implementation Status	Implementation Evidence (List and Submit Evidence)
The curriculum I follow is aligned to state and national standards and supports various student populations in my advanced level classroom (English learners, SPED, 504, 2e and 3e, Low SES, etc.)	☐ None ☐ Have An Awareness ☐ Planning ☐ Implementing	
The instructional practices I implement are aligned to state and national standards and support various student populations in my advanced level classroom (English learners, SPED, 504, 2e and 3e, Low SES, etc.)	☐ None ☐ Have An Awareness ☐ Planning ☐ Implementing	
I collaborate consistently with various stakeholders in my school/district to support the various student populations enrolled in my advanced courses (Co-Teaching, SPED, Counselors, PLCs, etc.	☐ None ☐ Have An Awareness ☐ Planning ☐ Implementing	

(Continued)

Element	Developmental & Implementation Status	Implementation Evidence (List and Submit Evidence)
I collaborate consistently with various stakeholders in my school/district to support the various student populations enrolled in my advanced courses (Co-Teaching, SPED, Counselors, PLCs, etc.	☐ None ☐ Have An Awareness ☐ Planning ☐ Implementing	
I communicate high expectations for each student with the needed support to match the expectation in all advanced level classrooms.	☐ None ☐ Have An Awareness ☐ Planning ☐ Implementing	
I use multiple data sources for behavioral and instructional support for decision-making (formal/informal assessments, progress monitoring, observations, coloration with other campus stakeholders, etc.) in my advanced level classroom	☐ None ☐ Have An Awareness ☐ Planning ☐ Implementing	
If a student has difficulty understanding lesson topics or objectives, I provide regular intervention opportunities to support students in the advanced level classroom.	☐ None ☐ Have An Awareness ☐ Planning ☐ Implementing	
Students are consistently engaged in coursework and feel valued and respected with the school community.	☐ None ☐ Have An Awareness ☐ Planning ☐ Implementing	

CRE SCORECARD

Category 1: Diversity, Inclusion, Equity & Justice Evidence/ Statements				
[Insert ranked score for: V, S, U, OR N] **The information and/or performance tasks …**	*How satisfied are you?*			
	V	S	U	N
Diversity 1. Are representative of multicultural perspectives and/or populations.				
2. Are presented in various modalities (graphics, verbal, logical, etc.) to facilitate perceptual thinking and understanding.				
3. Represent diverse identities as assets and strengths that can advance organizational structure, rather challenges or difficulties to be overcome.				
4. Develop bridges to connect cultural references to academic/occupational skills and concepts.				
CR Lens: Diversity Ranking Total	D(V) =	D(S) =	D(U) =	D(N) =
[Insert ranked score for: V, S, U, OR N] **The information and/or performance tasks …**	*How satisfied are you?*			
	V	S	U	N
Inclusion 5. Promote authentic representation and full participation of CLED groups.				
6. Show evidence of embracing and respect for differences without deficit.				
7. Do not include features that might lead to certain populations to dismiss the information for the wrong reason.				
8. Offer revisions to bias and isms.				
9. Build reader's cultural competence through learning about and developing pride in their own and others' culture.				
10. Engage reader in critical reflection about their own lives and societies.				
CR Lens: Inclusion Ranking Total	I(V) =	I(S) =	I(U) =	I(N) =
[Insert ranked score for: V, S, U, OR N] **The information and/or performance tasks …**	*How satisfied are you?*			
	V	S	U	N
Equity 11. Imply a guarantee of fair treatment, access, opportunity, and advancement.				
12. Do not maintain perpetual majority views for dominant cultures.				
13. Are free of debate or target of any people's humanity or dignity.				
14. Contribute to increase in number, retention and success and leadership for people of color.				
15. Enable students to be deemed proficient in completing the task even if expressing an atypical viewpoint.				
16. Prevent emotional stress as a consequence of representative isolation or separation.				
CR Lens: Equity Ranking Total	E(V) =	E(S) =	E(U) =	E(N) =
[Insert ranked score for: V, S, U, OR N] **The information and/or performance tasks …**	*How satisfied are you?*			
	V	S	U	N
Social Justice 17. Seek to correct imbalances of inequitable practices that stifle equal opportunities.				
18. Promote harm reduction and/or eradication (e.g. phrases - *affirms, challenges, protects, opposes, calls, demands, mandates, requires).*				
19. Are absent of cultural minimization and victimization.				
20. Do not maintain any dehumanizing views.				
21. Are not seen as individual problems but situated within a societal context.				
22. Assist reader to engage in critique of systems of power.				
23. Reduce the risk of disparate impacts on minoritized groups.				
CR Lens: Justice Ranking Total	J(V) =	J(S) =	J(U) =	J(N) =
Category 1 CR LENS Score: (All Lens Ranking Totals)				
NET Category 1 CR LENS Total *(Sum of Category 1 CR Lens Scores)*				

Category 2: Bias, Stereotyped & Fairness Evidence/ Statements				
[Insert ranked score for: V, S, U, OR N] **Check for Verbal Bias: The information and/or performance tasks …**	*How satisfied are you?*			
	V	**S**	**U**	**N**
24. Are absent of content that is different or unfamiliar to some CLED Groups.				
25. Do not include unnecessarily difficult language and vocabulary.				
26. Do not include unexplained group-specific language unfamiliar to different groups.				
27. Do not include undefined specialized words and vocabulary that may have different or unfamiliar meaning for different groups.				
28. Do not include reference pronouns that only certain groups might know.				
29. Do not include a format or structure (including directions and rubric) that may present greater problems for cultural groups than for others.				
CR Lens: Bias-Free Ranking Total	BF(V) =	BF(S) =	BF(U) =	BF(N) =
[Insert ranked score for: V, S, U, OR N] **Check for Stereotyping: The information and/or performance tasks …**	*How satisfied are you?*			
	V	**S**	**U**	**N**
30. Do not reflect a stereotypical view of, or offensive to, any CLED.				
31. Are not considered inflammatory, controversial, demeaning, offensive or emotionally charged for particular CLED group.				
32. Do not depict members of particular CLED group n stereotypical portrayals, occupations, or situations.				
33. Do not portray any CLED group as uniformly having certain aptitudes, interests, occupations, or personality traits.				
CR Lens: Stereotype-Free Ranking Total	SF(V) =	SF(S) =	SF(U) =	SF(N) =
[Insert ranked score for: V, S, U, OR N] **Check for Fairness: The information and/or performance tasks …**	*How satisfied are you?*			
	V	**S**	**U**	**N**
34. Include material that is equally familiar to all CLED.				
35. Portray each CLED group in a range of traditional and nontraditional roles.				
36. Represent CLEDs in proportion to their incidence in the general population.				
37. Include a balance of gender-specific and ethnic names, ethnic groups, and roles for each gender and ethnicity.				
CR Lens: Fairness Ranking Total	F(V) =	F(S) =	F(U) =	F(N) =
Category 2 CR LENS Score: **All Lens Ranking Totals**				
NET Category 2 CR LENS Total (Sum of Category 2 CR Lens Scores)				

Balanced Scorecard Metrics				
Net Category 1 CR Lens **Target** **Proposition Level**		*Net* Category 1CR Lens Total **Actual Score**		*Difference* *(Actual- Target)*
Net Category 2 CR Lens **Target** **Proposition Level**		*Net* Category 2 CR Lens Total **Actual Score**		*Difference* *(Actual – Target)*
Grand Total Actual Score Level = *Category 1 CR Lens Total + Category 2 CR Lens Total*				

CRE Prompt: *How satisfied are you with the cultural responsiveness of the document, information, content, and/or performance tasks?*

Ranking

V: Very Satisfied (+10 points)
If you are *very satisfied*, you should be able to provide an abundance of specific examples to show how and why the CR statement is accurate. It should be very clear that the text was designed to be culturally responsive. *Score this with positive ten points.*

S: Satisfied (+5 points)
If you are *satisfied*, you should be able to provide some evidence that the CR statement is accurate. The text may not have been designed to be culturally responsive, but evidence of elements of culturally relevance and responsiveness is apparent in most of the text. *Score this with positive five points.*

U: Unclear (-5 points)
If you are *unclear*, it is not obvious to you whether there is evidence to support the accuracy of the CR statement. *Score this with negative five points.*

N: Not Satisfied (-10 points)
If you are *not satisfied*, you have concluded that there is little or no evidence to support the accuracy of the CR statement. There is little or no evidence of cultural responsiveness. *Score this with negative ten points.*

Example

[Insert ranked score for: V, S, U, OR N] **The information and/or performance tasks …**	How satisfied are you?			
	V	**S**	**U**	**N**
Are representative of multicultural perspectives and/or populations.	+10			
Are presented in various modalities (graphics, verbal, logical, etc.) to facilitate perceptual thinking and understanding			-5	

References

Amaro-Jiménez, C., & Semingson, P. (2011). Tapping into the funds of knowledge of culturally and linguistically diverse students and families. *The Magazine of the National Association for Bilingual Education (NABE)*, *33*(5), 5–8.

Banwo, B. O., Khalifa, M., & Louis, K. S. (2022). Exploring trust: Culturally responsive and positive school leadership. *Journal of Educational Administration*, *60*(3), 323–229. https://doi.org/10.1108/JEA-03-2021-0065

Basnight-Brown, D., Janssen, S. M. J., & Thomas, A. K. (2023). Exploration of human cognitive universals and human cognitive diversity. *Memory and Cognition*, *51*(3), 505–508.

Brigandi, C. B., Weiner, J. M., Siegle, D., Gubbins, E. J., & Little, C. A. (2018). Environmental perceptions of gifted secondary school students engaged in an evidence-based enrichment practice. *Gifted Child Quarterly*, *62*(3)1–17. https://www.doi.org/10.1177/0016986218758

Brown v. Board of Education of Topeka, 347 U.S. 483 (1954).

Brown, E. F., & Rinko-Gay, C. (2017). Moral frameworks for leaders of gifted programs and services. *Roeper Review*, *39*(2), 121–131. https://doi.org/10.1080/02783193.2017.1289485

Byars-Winston, A. (2014). Toward a framework for multicultural STEM-focused career interventions. *The Career Development Quarterly*, *62*(4), 340–357.

Coffey, M., & Tyner, A. (2023). *Excellence gaps by race and socioeconomic status*. Thomas B. Fordham Institute. https://fordhaminstitute.org/national/research/excellence-gaps-race-and-socioeconomic-status

Collins, K. H. (2015). CI 5319 social, emotional, and cultural contexts of advanced development [Unpublished resource], Department of Curriculum & Instruction, Texas State University.

Collins, K. H. (2016). CI 5383 Mentoring across the lifespan course [Unpublished resource], Department of Curriculum & Instruction, Texas State University.

Collins, K. H. (2018). Confronting colorblind STEM talent development: Toward a contextual model for Black student STEM identity. *Journal of Advanced Academics*, *29*(2), 143–168. https://doi.org/10.1177/1932202X18757958

Collins, K. H. (2021). Redressing and neutralizing institutional racism and systemic biases in gifted education. In M. Fugate, W. Behrens, & C. Boswell (Eds.), *Culturally responsive practices in gifted education: Building cultural competence and serving diverse student populations* (pp. 85–104). Routledge. https://doi.org/10.4324/9781003234029

Collins, K. H. (2018). Confronting colorblind STEM talent development: Toward a contextual model for Black student STEM identity. *Journal of Advanced Academics*, *29*(2), 143–168. https://doi.org/10.1177/1932202X18757958

Collins, K. H. (2021a). Redressing and neutralizing institutional racism and systemic biases in gifted education. In M. Fugate, W. Behrens, & C. Boswell (Eds.), *Culturally responsive practices in gifted education: Building cultural competence and serving diverse student populations* (pp. 85–104). Routledge. https://doi.org/10.4324/9781003234029

Collins, K. H. (2021b). Culturally responsive evaluation scorecard (CRE Scorecard) [Unpublished resource, 2nd ed.]. Evaluation tool adapted from culturally responsive concept-based curriculum checklist (CR3C), CI 5359 Curriculum for Depth and Challenge. Department of Curriculum & Instruction, Texas State University.

Collins, K. H. (2022a). Gifted and bullied: Understanding the institutionalized victimization of identified, unidentified, and underserved gifted students. In F.H.R. Piske & K.H. Collins (Eds.), *Identifying, preventing and combating bullying in gifted education* (pp. 117–129). Information Age Publishing.

Collins, K. H. (2022b, September). Culturally responsive evaluation of NASA NGS. Presentation for NASA EPDC current and pending meeting [Unpublished report].

Collins, K. H., & Roberson, J. J. (2020). Developing STEM identity and talent in underrepresented students: Lessons learned from four gifted, Black males in a magnet school program. *Gifted Child Today*, *43*(4), 218–230. https://doi.org/10.1177/1076217520940767

Cotton, C. B., Davis, J. L., & Collins, K. H. (2022). See Me! Addressing the invisibility of gifted Black girls with other learning exceptionalities. In F. H. R. Piske & K. H. Collins (Eds.), *Servicing twice-exceptional students:*

Socially, emotionally, and culturally framing learning exceptionalities (pp. 171–181). Springer Nature.

Collins, K. H. & Kendrick-Dunn, T. B. (2022). Fostering cultural capital for recruitment and retention: A holistic approach to serving gifted, Black students in gifted education. In J. Castellano & K. Chandler (Eds.), *Identifying and serving diverse gifted learners: Meeting the needs of special populations in gifted education* (pp.150–163). Routledge.

Collins, K. H., Sangam, D., & Huling, L. (2022, June). Culturally responsive evaluation of NASA's OSTEM NGS evidence-based STEM products [Position Paper]. LBJ Institute for STEM Education and Research, Texas State University, *Research & Publications, 5*(7).

Cotton, C. B., Davis, J. L., & Collins, K. H. (2022). See Me! Addressing the invisibility of gifted Black girls with other learning exceptionalities. In F.H.R. Piske, K.H. Collins, & K. Arnstein (Eds.), *Servicing twice-exceptional students: Socially, emotionally, and culturally framing learning exceptionalities* (pp. 171–181). Springer Nature.

Davis, J. L. (2021, February 24). Dr. Martin Jenkins: Recognizing giftedness in the Black community. *NAGC.* https://www.nagc.org/blog/dr-martin-jenkins-recognizing-giftedness-black-community

Davis, J. L., Floyd, E., & Roberson, J. J. (2020). The 4 Rs: A new framework for teaching diverse learners. *Teaching for high potential.* National Association for Gifted Children.

Evans, A. E. (2007). School leaders and their sensemaking about race and demographic change. *Educational Administration Quarterly, 43*(2), 159–188. https://doi.org/10.1177/0013161X06294575

Fink J. (2018). How does access to dual enrollment and Advanced Placement vary by race and gender across states? *The Mixed Methods Blog.* Teachers College Columbia University. https://ccrc-tc-columbia-edu.libproxy.library.unt.edu/easyblog/access-dual-enrollment-advanced-placement-race-gender.html

Ford, D. Y. (2011). *Multicultural gifted education* (2nd ed.). Prufrock Press.

Ford, D. Y., Collins, K. H., & Grantham, T. C. (2022). Addressing gifts and talents, racial identity, and social-emotional learning regarding students of color: Challenges and recommendations for culturally responsive practice. In S. Johnsen, A. Cotabish, & D. Dailey (Eds.), *NAGC pre-K-grade 12 gifted education programming standards* (2nd ed., pp. 58–93). Routledge. https://doi.org/10.4324/9781003236863-3

Ford, D. Y., Grantham, T. C., & Collins, K. H. (2018). Giftedness, racial identity, and social-emotional learning: Challenges and recommendations for culturally responsive practice (pp. 87–102). In F.H.R. Piske, T. Stolz, C. Costo-Lobo, A. Rocha, & E. Vazquez-Justo (Eds.), *Educação de superdotados e Talentosos - Emoção E criatividade (Emotion and creativity in gifted education)*. Jurua Editor.

Ford, D. Y. (2013). *Recruiting and retaining culturally different students in gifted education*. Prufrock Press.

Ford, D. Y., Wright, B., Washington, A., & Henfield, M. (2016). Access and equity denied: Key theories for school psychologists to consider when assessing Black and Hispanic students for gifted education. *School Psychology Forum: Research in Practice*, 10(3), 265–277.

Ford, D. Y., Dickson, K. T., Lawson Davis, J., Trotman Scott, M., & Grantham, T. C. (2018). A culturally responsive equity-based Bill of Rights for gifted students of color. *Gifted Child Today*, 41(3), 125–129.

Ford, D. Y., Collins, K. H., Grantham, T., & Moore III, J. L. (2021). Equity-based gifted and talented education to increase the recruitment and retention of underrepresented students. In R. Sternberg & D. Ambrose (Eds.), *Conceptions of giftedness and talent* (pp. 141–161). Palgrave-Macmillan, Cham. https://doi.org/10.1007/978-3-030-56869-6_9

Ford, D. Y., Collins, K. H., & Grantham, T. C. (2022). Addressing gifts and talents, racial identity, and social-emotional learning regarding students of color: Challenges and recommendations for culturally responsive practice. In Johnsen, S., Cotabish, A., & Dailey, D. (Eds.), *NAGC pre-K-grade 12 gifted education programming standards*, 2 ed. (pp. 58–93). Routledge. https://doi.org/10.4324/9781003236863-3

Gay, G. (2000). *Culturally responsive teaching theory, research, and practice*. Teachers College Board.

Gay, G. (2010). *Culturally responsive teaching: Theory, research, and practice* (2nd ed.). Teacher College Press.

Grantham, T. C., Ford, D. Y., Davis, J. L., Trotman Scott, M. F., Dickson, K., Taradash, G., … Roberson, J. J. (2020). *Get your knee off our necks: Black scholars speak out to confront racism against Black students in gifted and talented education*. The Consortium for Inclusion of Racial Groups in Gifted Education (I-URGGE). https://t.co/g8yRuzbaS1

Gerken, M. (2022). *Coda: Scientific testimony, cognitive diversity, and epistemic injustice*. Oxford University Press.

Gentry, M., Whiting, G., & Gray, A. M. (2022). Systemic inequities in identification and representation of Black youth with gifts and talents: Access, equity, and missingness in urban and other school locales. *Urban Education.* https://doi.org/10.1177/00420859221095000

Gooden, M. A., Davis, B. W., Spikes, D. D., Hall, D. L., & Lee, L. (2015). Testing the waters of change: Applying a model of anti-racist leadership in a principal preparation program. Manuscript in preparation.

Gorski, P. and Swalwell, K. (2023). Moving from equity awareness to action. *ASCD.* Available at: https://www.ascd.org/el/articles/moving -from-equity-awareness-to-action.

Graves, S., & Mitchell, A. (2011). Is the moratorium over? African American psychology professionals' views on intelligence testing in response to changes to federal policy. *Journal of Black Psychology, 37*(4), 407–425. https://doi.org/10.1177/0095798410394177

Grissom, J. A., & Redding, C. (2016). Discretion and disproportionality: Explaining the underrepresentation of high-achieving students of color in gifted programs. *AERA Online, 2*(1), 1–15. http://ero.sagepub .com/content/2/1/2332858415622175 doi:10.1177/2332858415622175

Jenkins, M. D. (1936). A socio-psychological study of Negro children of superior intelligence. *Journal of Negro Education, 5*(2)175–190.

Johnsen, S. K., Haensly, P., Ryser, G., & Ford, R. (2002). Changing general education classroom practices to adapt for gifted students. *Gifted Child Quarterly, 46*(1), 45–63. https://doi.org/10.1177/001698620204600105

Johnsen, S. K., Simonds, M., & Voss, M. (2021). *Implementing research-based gifted education practices: An administrator's viewpoint.* Prufrock Press/ Taylor and Francis.

Khalifa, M. (2018). *Culturally responsive school leadership.* Harvard Education Press.

Ladson-Billings, G. (1995). But that's just good teaching! The case for culturally relevant pedagogy. *Theory into Practice,* 159–165.

Ladson-Billings, G. (1995). Toward a theory of culturally relevant pedagogy. *American Research Journal, 32*(3), 465–491.

Lakin, J. (2016). Universal screening and the representation of historically underrepresented minority students in gifted education: Minding the gaps in card and Giuliano's research. *Journal of Advanced Academics, 27*(2), 139–149.

Lockhart, K., & Mun, R. U. (2020). Developing a strong home–school connection to better identify and serve culturally, linguistically, and economically diverse gifted and talented students. *Gifted Child Today*, *43*(4), 231–238. https://doi.org/10.1177/1076217520940743

Michael-Chadwell, S. (2011). Examining the underrepresentation of underserved students in gifted programs from a transformational leadership vantage point. *Journal for the Education of the Gifted*, *34*(1), 99–130. https://doi.org/10.1177/016235321003400105

Moll, L., Amanti, C., Neff, D., & González, N. (1992). Funds of knowledge for teaching: Using a qualitative approach to connect homes and classrooms. *Theory into Practice*, *31*(2), 132–141.

National Association for Gifted Children. (2019). *2019 Pre-K-grade 12 gifted programming standards*. Author.

National Center for Educational Statistics. (2023, May). *Public school enrollment*. National Center for Educational Statistics. https://nces.ed.gov/programs/coe/indicator/cga/public-school-enrollment

National Center for Education Statistics. (2022). Racial/ethnic enrollment in public schools. *Condition of Education*. U.S. Department of Education, Institute of Education Sciences.

Novak, A., & Lewis, K. (2022). A methodological approach to designing a theory: The journey of the four zone professional learning model. *Roeper Review*, *44*(1), 49–62. https://doi.org/10.1080/02783193.2021.2005206

Olszewski-Kubilius, P., & Corwith, S. (2018). Poverty, academic achievement, and giftedness: A literature review. *Gifted Child Quarterly*, *62*, 37–55. doi:10.1177/0016986217738015

Paris, D. (2012). Culturally sustaining pedagogy: A needed change in stance, terminology, and practice. *Educational Research*, *4*(13), 93–97.

Park, V., Daly, A. J., & Guerra, A. W. (2013). Strategic framing: How leaders craft the meaning of data use for equity and learning. *Educational Policy*, *27*(4), 645–675. https://doi.org/10.1177/0895904811429295

Prasad, P. (2005). *Crafting qualitative research: Working in the postpositivist traditions*. M.E. Sharpe.

Professional Standards Committee. (2019). *2019 Pre-K-grade 12 gifted programming standards*. National Association for Gifted Children.

Qi, M., Armstrong, S. J., Yang, Z., & Li, X. (2022). Cognitive diversity and team creativity: Effects of demographic faultlines, subgroup imbalance and information elaboration. *Journal of Business Research*, *139*, 819–830.

Roberson, J. J. (2020). *The Voices of Leaders: Examining the underrepresentation of diverse students in Advanced Academic programs through a culturally responsive leadership lens*. Doctoral Dissertation. Texas A&M University-Commerce.

Roberson, J. J., & Floyd, E. F. (2020). Culturally responsive leadership and advocacy. *Teaching for High Potential, 1*, 14–15.

Roberson, J. (2023). Beyond Evaluation: Using Equity Audits for Advanced-Level Programs. *Gifted Child Today, 46*(2), 119–127. https://doi.org/10.1177/10762175221149442

Roberson, J.J. (2023). Breaking the glass ceiling: equitable leadership practices to help alleviate Gifted underachievement. In Collins, K., Roberson, J.J. and Fernanda, H. *Underachievement in Gifted Education: Perspectives, Practices and Possibilities*. Routledge.

Roberson, J.J. (2024). Utilizing Professional Learning Communities (PLCs) to Cultivate Equity in Gifted Education. *Teaching for High Potential. National Association for Gifted Children*.

Robinson, A. (2021). An administrators' association partnership translates to gifted education advocacy. *Gifted Child Today, 44*(1), 13–19.

Rogers, E. M. (2003). *Diffusion of innovations* (5th ed.). New York: Free Press.

Sangam, D., Collins, K. H., & Huling, L. (2023, January). Identifying and utilizing cultural Capital approach to implement culturally responsive strategies [Position Paper]. LBJ Institute for STEM Education and Research, *Research & Publications, 6*(1).

Shiel, T. (2017). *Designing and using performance tasks enhancing student learning and assessment*. Corwin.

Shields, C. (2010). Transformative leadership: Working for equity in diverse contexts. *Educational Administration Quarterly, 46*(4), 558–589.

Shields, C. M., (2013). *Transformative leadership: Equitable change in an uncertain and complex world*. New York: Routledge

The College Board. (2014). *The 10th annual AP report to the Nation*. The College Board. http://media.collegeboard.com/digitalServices/pdf/ap/rtn/10th-annual/10th-annual-ap-report-to-the-nation-single-page.pdf

The College Board. (2017). College credit in high school. Working group report. http://hdl.voced.edu.au.libproxy.library.unt.edu/10707/445592

The College Board. (2022). AP® cohort data report: Graduating class of 2021. https://schools.utah.gov/file/91cdf876-d30c-4e73-8fcf-ae9856794e9a

Tschannen-Moran, M. (2014). *Trust matters: Leadership for successful schools*. John Wiley.

U.S. Department of Education, Office for Civil Rights. (n.d). 2015–16 state and national estimations. https://ocrdata-ed-gov.libproxy.library.unt.edu/estimations/2015-2016

VanTassel-Baska, J., & Johnsen, S. K. (2017). Making change happen: Implementing the teacher education standards in the real world of education. In S. K. Johnsen & J. Clarenbach (Eds.), *Using the national gifted education standards for pre-k-grade 12 professional development* (2nd ed., pp. 155–169). Prufrock.

Varelas, M., Martin, D. B., & Kane, J. M. (2013). Content learning and identity construction: A framework to strengthen African American students' mathematics and science learning in urban elementary schools. *Human Development*, *55*(5–6), 319–339.

Wright, B. L., Ford, D. Y., and Trotman Scott, M. F. (2017). Multicultural pathways to STEM: Engaging young gifted Black Boys using the color-Coded Bloom-Banks matrix. *Gifted Child Today*, 40(4), 212–217. https://doi.org/10.1177/1076217517722577

Valencia, R. (2010). *Dismantling contemporary deficit thinking: Educational thought and practice*. Routledge.

Whiting G. W., & Ford, D. Y. (2009). Multicultural issues: Black students and advanced placement classes: Summary, concerns, and recommendations. *Gifted Child Today*, 32(1)23–26. https://doi-org.libproxy.library.unt.edu/10.4219/GCT-2009-840

Xu, D., Solanki, S., & Fink, J. (2021). College acceleration for all? Mapping racial gaps in Advanced Placement and dual enrollment participation. American Enterprise Institute. https://www.aei.org/research-products/report/college-accelerationfor-all-mapping-racial-gaps-in-advanced-placement-and-dual-enrollment-participation

Yang, Y., & Gentry, M. L. (2023). *Striving to excel in STEM: Insights from underrepresented, minoritized graduate students with high academic ability. *Gifted Child Quarterly*, 67(2)110–136. https://doi-org.libproxy.library.unt.edu/10.1177/00169862221119208

For Product Safety Concerns and Information please contact our
EU representative GPSR@taylorandfrancis.com Taylor & Francis
Verlag GmbH, Kaufingerstraße 24, 80331 München, Germany